KNOCK WOOD

Also by Jennifer Militello

A Camouflage of Specimens and Garments
Body Thesaurus
Flinch of Song
Anchor Chain, Open Sail

KNOCK WOOD

A MEMOIR

JENNIFER MILITELLO

DZANC
BOOKS

DZANC BOOKS

5220 Dexter Ann Arbor Rd.
Ann Arbor, MI 48103
www.dzancbooks.org

Library of Congress Cataloging-in-Publication Data

Names: Militello, Jennifer, author.
Title: Knock wood / Jennifer Militello.
Description: [Ann Arbor, Mich.] : Dzanc Books, [2019]
Identifiers: LCCN 2019013629 | ISBN 9781945814969
Subjects: LCSH: Militello, Jennifer. | Poets, American--Biography. | Women poets, American--Biography. | Dysfunctional families. | Man-woman relationships.
Classification: LCC PS3613.I53225 A6 2019 | DDC 814/.6 [B] --dc23
LC record available at https://lccn.loc.gov/2019013629

First US edition: August 2019
Interior design by Michelle Dotter

Printed in the United States of America

10 9 8 7 6 5 4 3 2 1

CONTENTS

Theory of Relativity	5
The Witnesses	9
Knock Wood	15
Dear Your Honor:	19
The Town	23
Duplex	27
All the Resonance of a Smashed Violin	33
Memory as the Quince	37
Knock Wood	39
On Fragility	43
The Problems of the Mothers	47
What to Leave, What to Unearth	55
On Time	59
The Mechanics	65
Knock Wood	69
Why I Became a Criminal	73
Latent Print	79
Procedures for an Outing	83

Invasive Species   87

Dead Reckoning   89

Knock Wood   93

The Living Room   97

Flower Girl   101

The Repairs   105

The Accidents   109

Conspiracy to Commit Larceny   115

The Deaths   119

Knock Wood   127

Vow   131

For all our selves, future and past

The time is out of joint.

—Hamlet

THEORY OF RELATIVITY

It was knocking on wood in 2016 that caused the death of my uncle three years before. I was on a plane from London, reading a Murakami novel about an uncle with cancer, and felt the need to knock as a protective measure against illness. But I had no wood. I figured paper was close enough, until I felt that ill-fated knock travel back through time. Uncle Jimmy was his name. He had been seventy when he died. He found out he had pancreatic cancer when he went to the doctor about foul-smelling stool, and he was dead three weeks later.

He had been abusive and insane, had gone after his wife with a kitchen knife, and had conned my father out of the money he was due upon the sale of his parents' house, so we cared as much as we could, but it wasn't that much.

From then on, I only knocked on actual wood. Recognizable wood. Presswood was okay. Sometimes I felt unsure whether wood was actually wood and would have to weigh the risk. But I already knew it was too late. I had knocked on a newspaper eighteen years before, while dating Harry, and now I was waiting to pay the price.

Harry had been a wreck. He dropped acid like it was going out of style. He drove trucks into trees without remorse. He was the son of a garbage collector and a country western singer, and the first time I saw him, he was passed out in the passenger seat of the cab of his stepbrother's pickup.

That summer, I was sixteen years old. The grass was growing long in the abandoned lots. Heat was rolling off the pavement in tongues, shimmering up from the blacktop. The rumor was there would be a blackout and people would die. Manhole covers steamed. Gutters clogged. Neighborhoods filled with men in their lawn chairs on the sidewalks at dusk and the shouts of children playing in the street. The rattle of air conditioners echoed from the windows. Construction workers took long breaks in the shade of their trucks.

I had been at a party with Sharon and Kevin, the friends who had sex in the back seat of the car while I drove, the ones who blew pot smoke into each other's mouths as they kissed, the high school sweethearts most likely to marry. Sharon had said about Harry, *He's trouble*, and I felt my curiosity stir.

When I pulled up to the house the night of our first date, he was out front with his arms elbow-deep in the guts of a car. The shadows were getting longer as he wiped his hands on a filthy rag and led me around to the back of the house to the big rabbit hutch there. The rabbits huddled together in the corner of the chicken wire enclosure. Their flattened ears were like remnants of velvet, and their back legs were tucked away like fists.

Harry plucked one from the cage, gathering it into his body, away from the wind. He uncurled the tightening comma of it as it worked to burrow into his shirt. There was a distance in its eye, as if it were at the edge of the sea. The eye looked blind as a marble, dark and shining at the center, without depth. Its nose shivered. The ear veins knitted lines through the thin skin like rivers.

I had read somewhere that they sounded human when they screamed.

When I asked the rabbit's name, he said it didn't need a name. I asked whether we could name it. I wanted to name it Hazel. Harry didn't answer.

He leaned down to see it, then suddenly took his hand and wrapped it firmly around the rabbit's face. He rattled its head until the animal squirmed and kicked, and then he released it back into the cage.

As we walked up to the house, I thought of the rabbits out there in the night hearing the voices of predators as the dusk set in and of the smells they could smell and how they must feel with no underground to get to. Each tiny rabbit heart ticking like a watch wild with time run away and gone. I had heard of wild dogs ripping rabbits from cages and snapping their necks and carrying them off into the woods, their hot mouths satisfied with the torn belly and meaty haunch.

When I went by Harry's house to say goodbye the night before I left for college—long after we had broken up—there was no one home. After ringing the bell, I walked around to the back of the house.

The pelt had been hung, stretched on a rack, and maggots crawled over it, cleaning it of flesh. Four solid pegs held it in place and its shape seemed obscene and exposed. Vulnerable. The late light filtered through the rigid membrane like the skin of a drum.

THE WITNESSES

She had been beaten by my Uncle Tommy in the apartment right below her parents' house. Her father would have heard the crashes and screams and yelling and muffled shouts. The punches he knew were landing on his daughter's body must have echoed through his sleep, violence as the soundtrack to his dreams. Even when he couldn't hear the shouts or the scuffles, he must have imagined he could hear them, must have strained to listen through the floor for a body falling against a table or dresser, or a crashing lamp that held an interruption of air like the sheets rustling as he turned. While the photographs on the wall rattled and loosened like teeth. While the moldings shook. While the clock ticked like fists being stiffened into place. While the walls braced themselves and the kitchen pilot light hissed and flickered like breath let from between curled lips. He'd think he'd hear an open palm slap across a face, but it'd just be the bread settling in its basket.

It was none of his business. He would lie on his back as his head hummed and the pillow was like a sea in that it magnified the sounds, let his daughter's screams travel in their slow deep way, resonate through the ear bones, resonate through the skull, carried in low frequency from the wild canyon of the mouth, from the throat's vibrato cave. He could not be more haunted if the sounds were ghosts.

It is none of my business, he would repeat to himself. She was married now. He would wrap the pillow around his head and try to keep the darkness from emphasizing the ticks of the kitchen radiator cooling down or the dead silence of the pages of books that took possession of the living room. Cars passed; their coming swish waned into their going. Rain fell and rattled at the windows. Snow came and muted the loudest of steps.

Still he would lie, through the seasons, guessing at the scenes downstairs, hearing the rage and the plates smash and the steps running for refuge or shelter. His wife would lie beside him deep in slumber. She slept on her side, facing away, and he would wonder at her peace. Somehow, she had been washed clean and made to dress each day and button each button and don each stocking and stir each pot and cook each meal and cluck when a glass was broken and scold when an item was left out of place. They were her words. It was she who would say, *It is none of our business.*

So he would sleep little and when he slept, he would wake thinking he heard what he did not hear, what had once been a baby crying in the next room—when he had risen to comfort her, tiny helpless wisp in his arms, and she had rested her dark-haired head on his shoulder as he crooned low and walked back and forth, smoothed her shock of hair and patted her knobbed back, and when she fell asleep again, lifted her as gently as he could down into the crib, arranging the blankets so that she was warm, lowering her there onto her belly where she slept best and gazing for a moment at her slack mouth and pinpoint of a nose, listening for her milkweed breath, closing the door gently so that the hinges stayed silent and the bottom of the door could ease over the carpet, and *let her sleep*, he would wish, *let her sleep.*

He would remember her in her bedroom barely a bedroom as a child, just a space behind a divider hardly big enough for a bed, as she sat cross-legged, surrounded by stuffed animals, listening to him remove his wingtip shoes, unsnap the garters on his socks, listening to her mother remove her makeup in the mirror across from their bed. He knew that when she dreamed, the breath of her parents rose and mingled with her breath, her sighs responded to their sighs, the same carpet lined their feet.

He would imagine this in the same way he imagined the husband of his daughter succumbing to rage and that rage eating at his liver like some mythological bird of prey.

Then she jumped in front of a subway.

Something no one in the family would admit.

I could imagine my aunt at the station, slim and stunning in her model's houndstooth coat—for she had been a model—her heeled leather boots, the wind up from the track, the edges of the coat flaring. When she jumped, I imagine her black hair fell lit and long, flung like a scarf. How those present must have felt the movement of the cars through the tunnel, heard the rumble, and leaned in anticipation, started to gather themselves, choreographed the preparatory steps and common bodily language that greets the incoming train. Newspapers were folded under arms. Briefcases were lifted. The sitting stood. The standing took a few forward steps.

How surprised they must have been as her shape flashed for a quarter second suspended in the air and the electric rail buzzed and sparked and her trajectory arced the way electricity does and she was down just before the rush of windows and faces slowing, fathers on their way home, children with their mothers, mothers with their strollers, a platform full of new wives and old women and homeless teenagers and businessmen in suits.

They would have removed their headphones and lowered their newspapers and clutched their babies close. First, the shock. Then they would have wondered whether appointments they must be present for would be missed.

The woman who had been to the hairdressers saying, *Think of the poor girl's mother.* The ones who couldn't wait to tell their co-workers. Couldn't wait to tell their husbands over dinner, as the man shoveled carrots into his mouth, *You'll never believe what happened today*—Those who couldn't wait for the suspense like telling a very good joke, they couldn't wait to be the center of that interest, the focused look, to hear the response and know that they had conjured it, the witnesses couldn't wait to look for it on the evening edition of the city news, they couldn't wait to cluck and judge and shake their heads, they couldn't wait to see the look on their wives' faces, they couldn't wait to tell anyone they saw, to start a conversation at the mini mart, to wow the Palestinian baker, to mention it at the laundromat.

They would say it and say it, again and again. For days. For weeks.

When Kathy woke, it would have been to an aura so white she must have thought it heaven. Coming up from the underwater she hadn't expected to rise from, emerging to a vague light and tubes and wires. The chair beside her bed would have sat empty. Instruments would have been ticking and breathing and beeping, and the bed sheets would have rustled with a tidal rush as she began to move.

Her mouth dry. Her limbs filled with lead. There would have been an IV taped into her arm, an embedded needle attached to a tube into which a clear liquid was dripping.

Kathy would have liked the quiet of the IV. The jotting down of dosages. Her meals coming. Her gown half tied in the back. The clean sheets and uniforms and the clean steps not followed by sound.

She could sit and look out the window. She could sit in stasis for hours, for days. She could float weightless through the ether of her thoughts and there was no pressure to be or talk or come back or exchange.

She would have slept when she wanted, and looked out the window to the building's other wing, accidently glimpsing the ill and the weak in their lit, visible rooms sleeping slack-mouthed or trying to rise from their beds. She could see the sky change and she could see the few flakes fall when it snowed.

It would have freed her, not wanting to live. The weight would have lifted a bit with the attempt. It was as if she had succeeded. As if she were dead.

The room's whiteness would have swallowed her. Its overhead lights and smell of snow. Its whiteness as a veil she could wear as she felt covered by some holy hour, felt like a drug in the room's vein. Like a floating curtain stirred by the breeze. The ease with which the nurses passed. Their own quiet miles of routine, their own quiet Mobius strip from room to room, from bed to bed.

Except she would soon have been pregnant with my cousin. Maybe she had been pregnant already, without knowing when she jumped. Maybe she found out she was pregnant while in the hospital. Maybe the doctor had come in, pulling the bedside chair closer to her bed and sitting, crossing his ankle over and resting it on his knee so that she could see the tight black knit of his sock. Leaning in toward her. Saying: *You are going to have a baby*. What. What then. What could possibly have happened next.

KNOCK WOOD

When I went to meet Tim on that first June night in New York, I knew that at last the punishment I was waiting for had come. He wasn't at the station when I got there, though it was 2 a.m. To make it easier, I was drunk.

When he finally showed up, he took me to his hotel, where we didn't kiss. At least not at first. I stood terrified in a corner while he talked. I could see the blue eyes I remembered from the one time we'd met before. I could hear the dark-current voice. I could feel the reasons I was there hiding down beneath my fear.

I knew I'd leave my marriage. I knew I'd regret it and die crazy. But none of that could be helped. The arrow points both ways. You wish for a reply and that causes the reply to be written in the future. You knock on a novel instead of wood and it kills someone in the past. The moment Tim walked into the train station, striding long strides, wearing a suit jacket with the buttons missing on one sleeve and wingtip boots, I remembered that other, former knock. Harry had been talking about the end of our relationship, I had touched the newspaper with my knuckles, and I knew then that that knock would echo into the future and end some relationship there. Or else my decision to get on the train that night had caused that knock in the past.

From the moment I met Tim, everything was a déjà vu. Every moment was a moment that had happened someplace else. I knew what to say because all I had to do was remember it. I knew wormholes opened when we walked through the cities. Boston. London. New York. I knew they closed up behind us as we slept. Sleet storms. Museums. Dinners. Drinks.

Maybe it's the act of being with another that marks time, since it's always seeping like rainwater into some unending ground.

Months passed. Years passed. I had known him before he was born.

We were twisted in the way we loved. We bit to show affection. We shouted to show respect. We broke furniture. We cursed. We injured one another. This was how we knew it was real. Our mothers had been cruel. We had learned we were worth little. The only way we knew love was through hurt. We gave each other the gift of harm.

Every time we left the bed, it would be covered with mildew when we returned, as if we'd been gone for years. Every time we left the house, we would tie a string to the door so that we could find our way back.

When he lied about his age, I knew he wasn't fastened to time the way the rest of us were. Because of this, he would disappear. I would catch glimpses of him beneath a cherry tree covered in blossoms in spring or trapped in a blizzard for days during winter. But we never stayed together for an extended period of time. We would come and go through the doors of our meetings as if always headed to another destination.

He always wore black. He said it was so that he'd be mistaken for his shadow. His beard always stayed the length of stubble, though it was never trimmed. Some said he was the devil, some said he was an angel. I alone knew the truth: that he was a human trapped in a purgatory built of his own fear of the world.

He could sing, and when he sang, the songs were transformed to tremors in my hands or the pressure in my blood. There was a viscosity to the air. He punished me with too much love because I could not be his. I could not share his time. He went missing when I looked for him. And I had my roots underground in another life.

When he went shopping for food, he would come back with nothing. In this way, he made it clear we should starve.

He carved me a ring of a fallen oak so that I would never again be without knockable wood.

Once we found ourselves outside an art museum, walking behind a man carrying a tuba. It was an instrument huge and lit and unwieldy, not being played but ready to be played. Music in its future and its past. It felt like an instrument of the present moment. It felt like all time in one curve of metal. A sculpture. A structure. A gleam. It felt like us. A reflective object carried to make music, but often not making music. Bulky. Twisted. As beautiful and oversized as the sun.

We looked at each other and understood. We would be together forever, lost in the maze of a shine like this, trying to escape like the notes to open air but never quite making it out.

The next day, Tim asked me if I wanted to get married. As he asked, a catkin from one of the trees in the city floated down and landed on the lapel of his coat. I took it as an omen and told him no. What is a catkin? Is it a serpent? Is it a seed? In that moment, it was both. I was drinking champagne, though it wasn't yet time for lunch. He understood that the no meant yes. He understood that I was rejecting the marriage that had happened in our past, the one I could remember but could not relive. The next time we were in London, we exchanged rings on the Millennium Bridge. The sun was setting. The Thames was calm. The dome of Saint Paul's set its own sun. When we returned a year later, the river was rough. It was like the catkin falling. It was serrating time like a knife. I wouldn't go near the bridge that time. I knew what the violence of the river meant.

When I turned back that first night in the station, already filled with regret, the train had left and I was alone on the platform. I felt the start of another life. I didn't know it yet, but Harry had died of a heroin overdose three days before I'd departed for that meeting. I felt my own suicide begin.

Dear Your Honor:

Of course I am guilty. I confess. I got drunk. I kissed Harry, who was not my boyfriend at the time. I drove him to Joe's house. Joe was my boyfriend at the time. I drove both of them to the quiet street and parked while they got out of the car. Their faces were lit for a second by the overhead light when it went on as they opened their doors.

What was the crime again?

I waited. I was drunk. The darkness, the fog, the lack of substance swallowed them. It swallowed their outlines first. It swallowed their voices last. It swallowed the trees where I waited.

After a time, they returned. I listened to the conversation they had about the cell phone, the radar detector, wondering if they could make a call, joking about how they could speed now without being pulled over. Would they sell the things? What would they use the money for? I thought about the taste of Harry's lips and how they had felt as we sat outside in the dark at the pond's edge.

It seemed like there were always reeds. Always still bodies of water.

I still loved Harry though he had been dating Heather, though we had been sitting in the dark together that way for weeks, a secret, outside near a whisper of reeds, among a tolerance of owls, down by the old grist mill, with its water wheel not turning, or down on the old Navy base with its toxic waters.

I still loved him.

I drove them to Joe's house. We dropped Joe off. I drove Harry to Heather's house. He held onto the stolen things. I did think of that couple sleeping, that couple who did not think they needed to lock their car doors at night, that couple not suspecting that these boys would be opening the passenger side door quietly, and taking their things and then going shapeless again in the dark.

(Does this look at all like the statement the state police took? Does that document still exist?)

Over five hundred dollars' worth. Larceny.

I dropped him off at the bottom of her driveway. I thought of her sleeping soundly in her bed, and wondered when she would first wake, and what he would first tell her, and what she would say before they both settled down again to sleep. I watched as he walked up. In my headlights, he was large. It seemed he was always a figure in my headlights. His shirt was white. His back was broad. He must not have planned to commit a crime that night or he would have worn darker clothes.

I thought of Joe in bed, trusting.

I thought back to the time when I was Harry's girlfriend. How he had fed me M & M's in his parents' living room, how we had listened to low music in the dark of his bed while his parents played live country music at the Oak Hill Tavern and his little brother watched late-night reruns one room over.

The first time we met he'd been passed out in the cab of his stepbrother's truck.

On our first date, we parked at the fairgrounds and drank beer in the front seat of an Escort. We walked in the fields holding hands.

What was the crime again?

When the police car started circling my block, I called Heather first. We were friends then. We had met up by chance a few months before at a backwoods party where we started spitting on people for fun. The difference was Harry loved her. The difference was everyone said she was ugly and rich. The difference was her mother let Harry spend the night in her bed. The difference was she had a crush on Jeb Shartner whose family owned the local farm, and when we would drive by at night after drinking she would lean out the window and yell his name into the wind, and I was in love with her boyfriend.

I called her and told her the car was driving around, circling, and slowing down at another house and slowing down at my house and circling again and then finally stopping and an officer was getting out and my heart was thrilled with the drama (would I tell on them?) and I had to hang up and the cop was at my door, tall with boots and imposing hat and some sort of decorative cord and I wanted to co-operate because I was that kind of person, not one of them in that moment, an upstanding citizen.

When I tried to talk to the officer in the car, he said it was better to wait until we were at the station. He meant it was better to wait until I had signed away my rights. When I got there, they told me, *Sign this paper on the dotted line and then we can tell you what's going on.*

Later, when I was out on personal recognizance, I would think to myself while walking in the mall or the grocery store, *I am out on bail.*

I had turned eighteen two weeks before.

So yes, I am guilty. I drove two boys to a location where they committed a crime. I did not inform the authorities. I knew they had stolen expensive objects from a sleeping stranger and I did not report this to the police. I suppose if transportation is help, I had to some degree even helped them.

However, there was no conspiracy involved. Simply my inability to separate myself from the danger of loving someone who did not love me. He is a criminal, yes, but you should see inside his life.

He is seventeen years old. His mother is never home. His father is married to someone else.

He will get Heather pregnant next year and she will have an abortion.

He will be arrested again and again, for domestic violence, for other larcenies, until his child-like blue eyes no longer set him free, until he is old enough to do time.

So yes, if it is a crime to be with two boys whose lives are already over and to love the wrong person and to be drunk at the wheel and to not care for the moment whether you live or die or are caught kissing your boyfriend's friend or your friend's boyfriend or whether you will face trouble from your parents when you get home or what the future holds, if it is a crime to love the outline of his hair in the dashboard lights and the feel of his hands on my neck and cheek, then arrest me. Send me to jail. I am the one you want. I have done it again. Serve me the sentence. I'll do the time.

THE TOWN

Drive with me. Through the town where I grew up. Down through the main thoroughfare with its vacant storefronts and lit tattoo parlors, with its fast food joints and its one sadly sloping trailer park, with the Chinese restaurant that was once a bank, and the Salvation Army, and the convenience store on the corner. Past the barber, past the crouched, claustrophobic middle school, past the church and on into neighborhoods, with their ranch houses and late marigolds and dented mailboxes, with their quiet streets and towering oaks, with their barely manicured lawns and barely middle class cars, their curtainless windows and small kitchens lit and seen through the big front pane.

This town is filled with boys who have already spent time in jail. With girls who fistfight in driveways over a spilled beer. With groups of kids who play pool until the small hours and pass out on some beat-up couch at the crack of dawn. They restore vehicles and transplant engines and stand in their driveways with other kids, hands in pockets, drinking Bud from a can. The knuckles of the boys who will soon be men tighten into weapons, and they strike one another with a desperate rage, an almost agreed-upon choreography of their culture. Moving as if in slow motion, hair flying, wrecking their vehicles against telephone poles and smashing beer bottles, sharing girls, stealing copper pipe from the walls of the abandoned projects, hitchhiking casually along the roads, their jeans tight, their T-shirts tattered, their way of ducking in and out of affections and yet sharing a bond with the others, men they hated, boys they shunned. They see themselves reflected in the eyes of the others and they all hate it, this game, this strife.

The fights keep them alive. The violation of the law keeps them alive. The way they drive late at night at top speeds through winding wooded back roads with the headlights off and the music turned up; it almost kills them and it keeps them alive.

The rage drifts quietly in most of them. They are rows of sleeping volcanos, the magma building, the top blowing, surprising even though it's clear it was there all along. Every fight is about this hot-blooded town and its dead-end boredom and its crazed race forward without looking back. It is about these boys who hit each other so as to come awake, so as not to think of their actual lives looming, their alcoholic mothers and coked-up fathers, their disabled veteran fathers who can't work, their rough-looking mothers who smoke too much and sit in the kitchen and mutter at anyone who passes, their toothless fathers who can't afford groceries and encourage them to steal money to buy booze, the velvet pictures of Elvis in their living rooms and their unneutered pets and the sheets hanging in their windows for curtains and the cars they wreck. It is about defending what they have at the moment whether it is rational or not.

The beatings by fathers they hardly know are buried deep. They have grown tough seeing their mothers leave when they were just skinny things standing at the screen door in their underwear and watching her drive off—while their fathers, passed out on the couch, snored. Drank themselves to sleep again as soon as they woke.

Some are already the fathers or mothers of children they didn't quite want. They punch the shoulders of their sons. They pinch the arms of their daughters. Then they are gone. Driving too fast. Finding the best way to bypass the law. Breaking into houses. Ripping off liquor stores. Slapping their girlfriends around. Taking the corner down on Quaker Road too fast there by the machine parts factory and its low brick wall. They drive their trucks into trees and walk away laughing. They peel out and burn rubber. They spin donuts in the parking lots. They drink cheap beer sitting on their porches while their babies crawl in the dirt. They blast their music and wear black T-shirts and camouflage pants and drive fast and drink too much.

They work at the factory. They work at the convenience store. They work as security guards. But mostly they don't work. They drive the run-down roads of their messed up town with its blank doorways and whitewashed windows. If you stand outside their duplexes, you can hear them yelling from the street. They live by the revved engine and die by the emptied bottle, are born into a lack of love. What do they want? What are they hiding? What is deep down in them driving and driving them even when they are out of fuel or out of road, even when they have reached the end or reached the intersection and cannot turn and so head out straight into the trees where the darknesses wait? Their living rooms smell of stale ashtrays and soured yeast. They are here; you can feel them, and in the next moment they are gone, standing trial at one another's funerals and asking what had happened and feeling all wrong.

What can any of us know of their lives? The sons they are, skinny in their belted jeans, heads hung and long arms, what do we know of their starved kittens and unpaved driveways and widowed mothers and diseased dogs? What do we know of their bedrooms, mattresses without sheets, fridges without food, sugar the one thing on the shelves, the one broken chair in the kitchen in which they sit and then lean too far back? Their thick black boots clunking on the linoleum floor. What is there to do but move forward and not be saved but stay afloat by coaxing themselves from one risk to the next? Keep the blood flowing with the thrill and threat and give and take of doing wrong, the song of it in their veins, when there is no refuge, no place to rest.

Then there will be nothing left. Love them and they will be dust that sifts through your fingers. Love the damaged, the despised, the crooked, the lost. They are your boyfriends, your friends, or your fathers. Love them and this is what you get.

DUPLEX

I helped my father clean out Kathy's apartment after it became clear
that she would not be coming home.

As I pulled in at the row house with the cutout brick designs on
the patio, I thought about how as a girl I would walk the half block
down to the corner where Nineteenth Avenue met Shore Parkway,
always skipping the cracks, always counting the fourteen bluntly cut
squares that made up the sidewalk, at Easter in a full formal coat that
buttoned at the neck, holding my father's hand, or alone with a stick
that I poked into the spokes of the fence, lamenting the one shat-
tered slab right before the block came to an end and the two places
where the maples muscled their way up in eruptions that cracked the
concrete long and sharply along the roots. I would walk down to
the water and peer at the cars passing on the bridge, just a few blocks
from the grocer who displayed fruit on the sidewalk in boxes and
crates, just blocks from the old radio repair shop and the fish store
with all the dead fish laid out in a line, their milky eyes silvery on
ice. The yard was overgrown now. It had the air of a dwelling where
no one lived.

I smacked open the screen door and found myself there in the
gloom of my grandparents' house, among cardboard boxes my father
had gathered for the packing of the apartment downstairs, in a cur-

tained room daylight would never reach, with its stench of old encyclopedias, the smuggle of carpet still at the throat, the window with
the bulk of the television at one corner beside the old clock plodding
through the hours.

I walked out and down the stairs to the basement rooms. Most of
the furniture was still there, though it was obvious no one had used
it for a long time. The place was entirely intact, like a house made of
wax. Dust had gathered on the horses grazing in the vast tapestry that
covered one living room wall. Twin end tables and a coffee table were
set up around a space that had once held a couch. In the bathroom,
the bowl of the toilet had gone dry.

When I switched on the fluorescent light in the kitchen, it blinked like the eyes of someone woken from sleep, squinted and finally
lit, giving off an unnatural greenish hue that reminded me I was underground. The Formica table still cowered in the corner. The spoons
slept nestled in the drawers like children that could not wake. There
was a throb to the light of the refrigerator door. The dishes stacked
in the drainboard gleamed, and the pilot light still flared beneath the
burners of the stove. If I stood on tiptoe, I could see the backyard
through the window behind the sink, a wild place that once had been
tame, with the sloping form of a rusted swing set and the tangled
arrays of abandoned swings and old olive trees twisted like fingers
among the weeds taller than I was and thin as ghosts.

The bed in the bedroom was tidily made, the itch-rough fabric
of the polyester bedspread patterned with dark triangles and waves.
Matching curtains hung from the windows. The many photographs
I thought I remembered were gone from the dresser, but the old
presswood furniture remained. There were drawers filled with socks
and folded shirts and closets filled with clothes that no longer held
a scent. There were shoes neatly paired. Size four thin-legged jeans,
slim black button-down tops, shiny platform shoes manufactured for

tiny feet. And beside them the floral tops and balloon-legged pants of a woman many sizes larger.

The plywood drawers shuddered with being opened and shut. I pulled the shoulders of blouses from their hangers and unclipped slim skirts from their organized racks. I took down the heavy patterned curtains. I removed the bedspread from the queen-sized bed. I emptied shelves stocked with food, drawers filled with screwdrivers and new batteries and bracelets and toothpaste. I fingered small rings and folded dish towels and packed away the fashionable shoes. I dusted off the most cliché of trinkets, puppies and kittens and men bowing at the waist to women in petticoat dresses. Flatware and utensils, cleaning products, even a few old shirts Uncle Tommy had left behind. The plastic flowers from a vase in the bathroom. Rolls of blue toilet paper stacked under the sink. Aspirin and cough syrups and half-empty boxes of Q-tips and old congealed hair gels and shampoos. I dusted off picture frames with faded photographs of my cousin as a baby and as a grinning, toothless child, a picture of my aunt and uncle on their wedding day, wrapped them in newspaper and lowered them into liquor store boxes.

I was in one of the pictures, standing beside my cousin. We were at Nellie Bly, posing among passing strangers, before a scene of bumper cars and spinning teacups. She wore jelly shoes and a pink frilled T-shirt that said *Sweet*. It had been years since I'd last seen her. What had it been like for her? By the time she was six, she and her mother spent most of their time upstairs in my grandparents' house. Had she learned to watch her mother for warning signs or shifts in mood, as I had during our visits, the way one watched the sky for storms? Had there been a day when she returned from school to find her mother gone?

I moved on to the kitchen. Out the back window, the ivies climbed the walls and invaded the rusted swing set where the swings hung listlessly. Various ragweeds and crab grasses bristled thigh high and made the yard impassible. The olive trees, neglected and bare, gnarled up, and I remembered my grandfather trussing them in burlap for the winter, tending them with clippers and mulch, and plucking the olives once they grew ripe. I remembered him pruning back the bushes along the edges of the yard. I remembered the green mown grasses we would run out onto, sidling along the house in the narrow section that went to the front yard, where the neighbor's statue of the Virgin Mary sat. We would clamor under it and scoot out and scare one another and laugh. Back in the days when my grandparents' sisters and brothers would come for Sunday dinner, along with more distant cousins I would see just a few times a year but who would immediately meld into a pack of children running and tearing their Easter dresses on the thorns of the roses lining the walk, scuffing their shoes on the harsh cement of the poured concrete steps. Skinning their knees and scraping their elbows. We would come in wild and out of breath, with twigs in our hair, to sit down around the table in the small kitchen and gulp a glass of milk and eat an Italian cookie with colored sprinkles from the bakery down the street.

And then, as I aged, those Sundays faded, as the families broke down into smaller units and moved out of the city or married off or filled their Sundays with other things. Until it was only the immediate family that gathered, and there were so few of us that "gathering" was hardly the correct word. I would sit on the top step of the front stairs and toss pebbles down or sit in the back just past the screen door, and pull out grass by the roots and collect little piles of it. And then I grew too old for even that. So I sat on the plastic-covered couch and tried to make half-talk with the adults, but mostly by then it was waiting for the visit to be over, sitting at the table under the loud clock and nibbling a biscotti while the adults talked and had coffee, waiting for the mumble of voices and scrape of chairs pulling back that said everyone was leaving and time was up.

My aunt would never return, but she hadn't known that when she left. This much was obvious from the way things sat untouched for years. I realized that even my grandparents had not hoped for, but had believed in, her return. Or maybe part of them had believed she was still there, even as the water in the toilet evaporated and the utensils fell into a decades-long sleep and the horses stilled inside the tapestry. The clothes like mummifications in their drawers, like the preserved bodies of youthful pharaohs or Egyptian queens, embedded with jewels. They too had believed in an afterlife, a reincarnation. These blouses and jeans were the only remnants of the body of a woman sane and thin, beautiful and real. That woman was dead. It was her ghost who lived in the halfway house on Cropsey Avenue.

ALL THE RESONANCE OF A SMASHED VIOLIN

The girl runs because she loves to run, and because she loves to run, all the boys chase her. Her best friend is the tallest girl in the class. Her worst enemy is Donna Pedrosa, whose last name has changed three times and who lets the boys kiss her. The girl hates when her mother makes her wear her hair off her face. She has a parakeet that will die when she is thirteen. The same year her appendix ruptures. This year, to learn about ancient Egypt, her class makes a life-sized mummy from papier-mâché.

They have a watermelon seed spitting contest the last day of school.

Her father's wife is the kind of woman who pinches a child when no one's around just to see what the child will do. She dyes her hair but claims she doesn't. She has the body of a man; this is maybe the reason she never wears dresses. She loved her elderly cat, she claims, but she let him out late one night when he was sick and he never made it back. She dated a married man for ten years; when he broke up with her, she sent him receipts for every single gift she had ever given him, including a washer/dryer set, with a note that said if he did not pay her back, she would tell his wife everything. Once she got drunk on Nyquil and called people late at night, leaving messages to lament that the singer she loved did not win the reality show he was on. She did not know she had done this until the people called back. She lived with her mother well into her forties. She's afraid of flying. She's afraid of elevators. She's afraid of subways.

When the girl says his wife is odd, her father says, *What?*, like he's never heard the word before. The wife sleeps fifteen minutes at night on the chair in the TV room and has ADD and won't take medicine; the girl's father says the medicine will change who she is, which are her exact words. He pretends to like the Red Sox because his wife is obsessed with the team and it doesn't cost him to pretend.

Doesn't the girl want snow to change to rain so that roads don't coat with ice? Doesn't she want the laughter of children to turn into the petals falling from dogwoods? Doesn't she want the echoes from thunder and soot from a fireplace and electrons murmuring and clouds' magnetic fields?

At the same moment as her mother is going on a date with the man who will become a famous meteorologist, her mother is driving away from the hospital while her own mother is inside dying, because the stubborn woman won't die with everyone around her and she doesn't know what else to do.

What if this story were an elevator? Press a button: first floor. On the first floor lives the super who broke into the girl's grandparents' apartment once they had died and stole thousands of dollars in cash because he had harbored years of anger at the fact that their rent-controlled apartment had been theirs since they were young. On the fifth floor, the apartment itself. The great bedroom with the double white doors that swung in but didn't quite close unless you secured them with several thick green and red rubber bands. The bathroom so white your teeth were like dun in the mirror, with a cracked marble toilet paper dispenser and the hot pink cabinet filled with Q-Tips and creams, with the vatted doors that slid back, and its hot water pipe that got so hot you couldn't touch it without being burned. Its ceilings so cracked they seemed to spell something out, they seemed to go hand in hand with the sounds of car horns and sirens rising up from five floors below and the wrought-iron fire escape that curled up into itself while sleeping like an iron-boned snail. Cracks that went hand in hand with the moment the man on the bicycle in the street below was hit by a car or the spot at the corner where the water main was once exposed.

If the girl's mother were a character, she would be the controlling woman with the miserable husband. She has thrown away her husband's dead father's flannel shirt because it no longer fits him. She has given him the look she gives her children, the one where her lips twist up and wrinkle and deflate until your mouth stops saying, your heart colds over and you know that you have done something very wrong and that you will pay the price.

When this story begins, there is a woman at the wheel of a car. The sun is setting. The radio is playing a song she can remember. Her country is at war. She takes her foot off the gas and the car slows. She is alone on this stretch of highway and the car is filled with words sung sweetly or plaintively and she is alone. She stops the car by the side of the road. She gets out to watch the last of the light vanish from the hood and from the sky. She lights a cigarette. She forgets the way to the ocean. She forgets the name of her husband. She forgets the latitude and longitude of the town where she grew up.

Not far off, the desert she has dreamt of evolves into the highway. The rattlesnakes evolve into stones. The ocotillo evolve into saguaro. Her footsteps evolve into the echoing blurs. The future is her maze. Her blueprint is a smattering of stars.

Memory as the Quince

Memory makes worse worse, thieves steal, butchers bring corpses back to life, rain clear up, events begin just as they end, the fallen get up, the slow go quick.

Memory makes bone last longer than flesh, makes imperfection the norm, makes storms clear, makes evidence tell the exactly right truth. Makes the mind scatter, makes the mind bend. Empties the cemetery, grooms the landscape, preaches the sermon, stirs. Looks for flaws, finds photographs of families, finds instances of sanity, identifies abdomens one can probe for clues.

This is its tree, heat in the heart, beat in the thumb, pulse in the wrist: its nod is a quiet water I pole out onto. Its spine is a clock hand, its breeze is a bellows I use to soften metal at its bend. This is its tree, dropped rot at its foot I stoop to collect, and I think cider is a breath I never took, the me underneath the me, the voice underneath the bloom.

Memory makes worlds chalked on sidewalks, words free of their books, makes spines curve, makes weddings ruin. Memory makes sidewalks torn by trees, evenings dwindle, sacrifice happen, belief leave. Fences in endings, speaks of light. Craves rows of sinking ships, lisps when it speaks.

This is the fat crease along the bulb, slice at the seam where seeds web out. Cherry stone fuzz like a navel's fold, scold like a holiness or stem, shed velvet ribbed along its thread, star where dirt gathers, palm lines bled. Memory like an old line cut free, petals shed, petals brown. Where the ground digs itself in, scaled with cat graves, scaled with weeds, scaled with rocks that blunt the mower blades, woven with the rabbit's nest hidden in its length. A tree like a laugh bent far out of the past and casting its clogged gutters again toward rain. I live in its clapper, hung as a locket, copper as a clasp. I live in its bonnet, a bee bothered, mad for the hive.

Memory: a windowsill where owls roost, their bodies shaped like vases we fill with flowers cut at the stem, knowing they will die within days. Filled with a housefly's gaze, so many things at once. Cliffs from which we could leap. Who knew it would leave us like this.

This is its quince, bigger than the fist that is my heart. This is its quince, sour in the chest, crisp flesh or scar tissue, jellied into jars. This is its branch, grasp of skin or groan of bark split with the sunk section of rope. Brim over which I spill, sin over which I fret: this is the trunk with years one can count or flowers one mistakes for the coming of fruit.

KNOCK WOOD

With Tim, days grew into weeks. Weeks grew into years. He smelled like a forest until I smelled like a forest. He would rehearse combinations of our names. I felt like love had become a breed of venomous spider; we'd remove the poison to keep it as a pet. But in this spider, the venom grew back. It would bite and we would die, then it would bring us back to life.

We fought violently. I punched him. Once we yelled at one another in a café until I turned to walk away and he grabbed me by the arm and forced me to kiss him on the mouth. At last I had grown blind. Or learned to see. Or learned to see with my eyes closed. Or learned to use blindness to walk.

I couldn't keep the growl of us contained, or the howl, or the yell. We wouldn't keep quiet in my body. I would go back to my life after finding him in between some hour or month, and pace and move restlessly and push back, even as I raised children and loved them more than I loved myself.

We were both formed by the fires of a mother's hatred, armored with an inability to love; like pangolin, we wore our golden chain-mail and yet were soft, endangered within. A therapist of mine once called us two fetuses in a silo, which most perfectly made us twins.

But inevitably the return of the punishment had come. I had trusted a newspaper, that temporary husk of wood, with my fate. I had knocked not on the heart or pulp of some willow or birch, but on a bird of a thing, a hollow bone printed with words of a single day, with ink that smeared the fingers and then the face, a thin wisp of a page filled with horrors, cast aside half read, barely perused. I could feel that moment reawake every time Tim and I kissed. I could feel my knuckle against the cartilage-thin scrap. I could feel the panic in needing to guard against a future of loneliness, so that I was now trapped in a love that was like a dungeon in the way it owned me and hunted me down.

My husband didn't know. He didn't care to know. We grew apart. We pretended for the sake of the children, but we stopped sharing a bed and then stopped sharing a house. More and more my marriage felt like a limb deprived of blood, one that is still present but has grown cold and then goes black. The necrosis of my one life meant the turgid awakening of the next. I was riding the crest of a new thing. It was good the way a meal is good when you have already declared yourself full.

At the end of every visit, Tim would ask when we would be together. Then the mother in me closed up. I would imagine my children in a safe place and would keep them there in my life and in my gut. Nothing could endanger them. But I was torn apart. I would forget who I was while walking. I would wake up and piece myself together, starting with my name. I forgot where I lived. I forgot the names of my parents. Slowly I was being erased.

We were in a hotel room in Seattle when he told me he would kill himself if I ever left him. He said he would swallow pills. He had just given me the crystal ball that had belonged to his psychic grandmother, a woman who told people's fortunes for money. I took the ball in my hands and traced the scores along its surface. It fit

perfectly in the hollow between my hips. I cradled it there. I looked
out the window. Seagulls flew up between buildings like smoke. Like
smoke, I watched my future disappear. My children. My husband.
Any semblance of choice. When I looked back to it, the room had
been upended in the globe.

From then on, I dragged my feet. I cursed and spit. I dished
out hate. Until the day I realized I needed him, too. Until the day I
remembered he was in my blood. Except I didn't have to remember
it, because, with him, the present was the future. So I passed again
through events that had already happened. I walked again in the sunlight that had already shone.

The need continued. The need the need the need the need. I was
always two people and was never myself. I was running a race I could
never win. I would board the plane again and again, take my seat,
strap myself in. The plane would take off. The plane would land. I
would descend into London, New York, Boston, Seattle, Toronto,
Washington, D.C. I would endure jet lag and turbulence and con-
fusion and fear. Tim and I would walk and walk and see sights and
clock the miles of the sidewalks and sleep and wake and forget which
city we were in.

In this way, I killed my uncle. In this way, I killed myself. I
knocked on wood when someone mentioned sickness or death or
misfortune or loss of love. I was always trying to reshape the future
that was actually the past. I was always trying to undo what had already been done.

One day, I almost lost my sanity on an estate in Bath. I'd been
drinking all day while wearing a red and black silk dress and Tim
and I lay on the ground and the sky was blue and the grass was
green and there were sheep feeding off in the distance, where the
horizon met the white and perfect clouds. I felt the distance. I felt
the miles. I felt my children crying in their beds. I felt them asking

for me: *Mommy*. I felt their small bodies without my body beside them. I felt them asking. *Where is she? Why isn't she here?* Meanwhile, Tim took photographs of my splayed limbs, the contrasting colors, my lips swollen from kissing, my chin against his beard. I rose and my wine glass was empty. So I threw it beneath the tree limbs that were so thick and low they were rooted to the ground.

I was crying. I was inconsolable. There was a loss scissoring in me that could not be quieted. Tim followed the string back to the house and creaked the old wooden door open and cleared the spiders away and stroked my hair until the smell of the wild garlic calmed me. Then while I was sleeping, he went outside and paced and paced. When I woke, it was no longer day. He lit a fire and we sat before it. There were still streams of dried salt left by the tears along my cheeks.

I was lost, like the wine glass I'd abandoned and cast off. I felt alone and empty. I thought of the glass. I wondered at the species of tree. I wondered at the mowing of the field. I wondered at the peacocks that wandered the estate. The glass, like an eye in which the sky is caught. It would stay there like a grave marker, or like a skeleton of something that couldn't die.

Two years later, Tim would return and try to find that glass. I imagined it tilted against the ground and half filled with dirt. I imagined it holding onto that emptiness. I imagined it turning the rain that fell to a microscope slide of tears.

That day I knew I could never keep my balance. I was on the tightrope now, strung between the concrete and steel of two tall buildings, but eventually I would fall.

I knew the day would come when I would have to let myself die. I didn't have to knock on wood for that.

ON FRAGILITY

Kathy's daughter was born with blue eyes so translucent that the moody gray rims circling the irises made one think of faint haloes that formed around the sun. Once the baby was done with a raging, hiccupping introduction to the world, her face blinked shut so that her expression closed and softened like fruit found bruised on the ground. She took on a squint that would slowly pull open as the days passed, until she emerged a nun-like, round-faced baby girl unruffled as a lake and whose eye color recalled photographs of the distant earth taken by astronauts in the soulless expanse of space.

On the day Kathy brought her home and placed her in the small bassinet that had been set up in the living room, she must have felt at once thrilled and terrified. Lowering her into the soft bed, holding her breath. Remembering to keep one hand behind the baby's neck. Shifting the little bundle up onto her shoulder and lightly patting her back. She would have felt the tiny body relax against her; it was like holding a sack packed with cloth. This baby that couldn't move. This baby that couldn't feed itself or bathe itself or even lift its head. The thought of this froze something in her blood. How could she keep such a creature alive?

She wouldn't sleep that night, or the next. She pulled blankets far from her daughter's infant face. She watched for the rise and fall of the chest over and over, all night, every night, so that even those snatches of sleep her daughter got, she refused for herself. She looked at her child curled like a feather at the corner of the crib and thought of the disturbance of breath. She would wring herself out all night long with thoughts that circled around and around, the same thoughts rutting a sinewy path from one part of her brain to the next until she was nothing but that checking up on and doubling back. She was feed the baby, be sure the baby doesn't choke, burp the baby so the baby doesn't choke, watch the baby so the baby will wake, wake the baby to be sure the baby will wake, then that whole cycle again. Again. Again.

She would have waited for the smell of smoke. The sounds of a killer breaking in. She could feel the locks on the windows untwisting or the glass being cut. The hand reaching through. She could feel the blankets conspiring to suffocate her daughter. She could feel the food fatten in her throat and all the ghosts of illness knocking at her blood, all the germs being sucked into her lungs. All the blood-streams polluted. All the machineries of the body working against her as she tried to keep this whimpering half-being with a skinny little chest and curled, too-long alien fingers alive. Those moments she did not feel love; she felt the rest of her withering, dried leaf beneath the magnifying glass, heat of the sun multiplied within the beaming, fixed glare of its astringent eye.

Motherhood made her lose her sense of time. It made her feel watery and lost. Her bones felt like they were made of wool. Like they were made of wood. Like they were made of live wire. Made from steam rising off the radiator which lurched and knocked against the wall just inside the apartment door. They were made from the riverbed of voices she could hear from upstairs as it trickled down through the crooked vents and hot water pipes and miles of interior wall space. Her bones were museum bones though she was still alive.

They had been shellacked though they were still in her skin. They had been transformed to fossils, then had been sipped of their marrow; they had sunk in mud and lain there for thousands of years. They had turned to glass. They had a touch of rot.

When she sang to her daughter, she imagined the songs contained a voodoo recipe for sleep: skin of a poison dart frog, sting of a fire ant, dried human bones ground by moonlight into dust. Her hair was falling out; she would find thick clumps of it in the bristles of her brush. Her teeth felt raw and untethered in her mouth. Her arms trembled and grew weak and her legs could no longer bear her weight. She didn't have time to wash her face or get a slice of bread and chew it down or get up from the couch that sat under the high windows, making her feel like she was underwater, far from some impossible surface she relied on for air. Oxygen was vacuumed from the bedroom. The furniture trembled when she paced. Holding the baby, trying to get her to sleep. Not holding the baby, but working the white-capped foam of her thoughts into a frenzy. Boiling water for another dinner of spaghetti on the miniature burners; the pilot lights licked and licked in the night and, with a mere breath of gas, spread up to become a blue crown of thorns. She felt this innately, that she kept the family alive and fed them meals cooked by the heat of her suffering.

She touched the flame with her finger once to be sure the flame, or maybe the finger, was there. The tiny hairs between knuckles curled back and browned and disappeared; she could smell the singe, the edge of her fingernail turning the color of teakwood and smoking and then thickening in its melt. She turned the burner off and watched the light go back to its small snake tongue, small taste of air, small flick of blue, small snicker of need to be fed on something always, and always an eye, waiting to incinerate the house.

The Problems of the Mothers

The mothers didn't starve purposefully; the sons and daughters ate like hatchlings from their mouths. The children ate the bread baked and left each mother without a crumb. They ate the hens that died in the blizzard before she could boil them free of feathers. They fed at her inability to walk across the yard. They drank rainwater from the cistern and sipped her salted weepings, sipped her sugary blood. They grew and grew, but still demanded to be suckled to sleep so that she had to lie contorted beside them. They cried until she gritted her teeth. They clung to her until her hair fell out in clumps that resembled the petals of dogwoods past their season. Their cries carried through the ventilation and escaped into the rooms through ancient wrought-iron grates.

The mothers' hands grew more civilian each day. Their hands bittered to weeds in an overgrown garden. Their hands reflected wounds which were fatal, wounds they couldn't feel. Hours were unwelcome as guests. Voices reigned in their heads while they fought them and then let them ricochet as if their interiors were empty. The acoustics were healthier that way.

The mothers gathered at the banks of a river and dipped themselves in in the hopes of rendering their skins like iron since the battle would be a battle for years. Instead, they found themselves weeping at their unkempt reflections and at a sense of communion with the moving waters. They felt free of the little hands and mouths that haunted and crippled and pursued them; they felt moved by the natural sounds. The rivers spoke of baptisms, when there had been hope, and an imagined infant that had little to do with the real. Before the loss of sleep. Before the loss of all they could call themselves. Before the hunger that had the gnaw not of a single rodent but of all the rodents, numberless as rain. Their memories were like endless telephones ringing. They worshipped and got clean before they fell where they stood.

They walked a few steps along rutted roads that resembled their desiccated veins. Their spines bent. Their abdomens trembled. Before they were dead, they all had been ghosts. This was where the flesh came in; it had an end, like a rope.

When the children could not pass stool, the doctors told the mothers the pain was within normal range. When the children could not keep the room still, the doctors told them children turn and turn. When the children could not smooth their chests, the doctors told the mothers bones grow and the ribs break through and the shapes of things lose their symmetry and caliber. When the stomach spasmed, go home. When the breath was labored, go home. Go home. Sleep. When the fevers came, go home. When the vomiting emptied the small stomachs and the crying emptied small lungs, go home go home. They cannot eat they cannot sleep they cannot drink they cannot see. Go home go home go home.

The mothers developed ulcers in the palms of their hands and chapped sores at the roof of their mouths. Their hair filthy. Their thoughts flatlined like the pulses of the dead. What others said did not impress them, what others said could not reach their ears. The mothers could not feel joy. They could watch their children like stone. They could watch through the layers of watching and could not be sure what they saw. A smile into a small hand. A secret curl. A dark eyelash down over the pale and perfect cheek. A sigh at least. They could give a sigh. *Mommy,* the children said. A sigh in return.

The mothers would hold the little bodies and try to remember joy. They would know the bodies from their bodies. They would remember the moment the bodies had been lifted from their bodies and the one had become two and the fast heartbeat and the slow heartbeat had come together in the outside world. Now. That was a moment. The skin against the skin. The elbows of the knees pushing out and the stitchless thread of the mouth.

Before the handbags beneath the eyes held only blindness. When being responsive all night was good.

The instruction books talked about putting the baby down but the baby could not be put down. The instruction books talked about putting the baby to sleep. The baby did not sleep. The instruction books talked about singing to the baby. There was no song that would shut it out. The instruction books talked about taking time for oneself, but there was no time, or self. The mothers began hallucinating: the baby unbuckled, the baby unfed, the baby lost. They saw the baby being held by other women, women it did not know, women who could not feed it or say its name. They saw the panic in its eyes, but could not take it back.

They saw their own mothers as babies. They saw their own mothers as mothers are, crushed. The mothers didn't know they should settle for less. There was still something inside them that aspired to thinking or sitting or looking at trees. The mothers squirmed among the melted popsicles and skinned knees, among the open-mouthed raging and the meals to be made and the lack of talk and the gastro-intestinal distress. Breakfasts rejected. Lunches ignored. Clocks that moved too slowly. When morning hatched, it was an egg that birthed the realization that dawn could be just as dark as any other hour, and that things were not going to change.

What the mothers didn't know repeatedly hurt them. Whether the child was taking a breath. Whether the blankets had covered its face. How small to cut the food. Whether it was a tooth. Whether it was gas. How clearly to say the word. What to invent. What to make true. Whether the cold would cure the cough, whether the bath was too hot, whether the baby could see underwater, whether another mother would feel this or not. The babies proved unable to stay asleep. The mothers wrapped their babies in newspaper so they would stop crying but not be silenced, they hovered their babies over balconies so they would fall but not too far.

The instruction books were inflexible. Let the baby pull your hair. Let the baby eat your heart. Do not let the baby sleep too long. Do not let the baby put things in its mouth. Watch the baby so that it does not fall from the chair/couch/floor/bed/car. Watch the baby so that it grows used to being watched and cannot be alone. When you cry in desperation, do not make any sound. The mothers were mannequins of nod and smile. Their ability to hear grew so keen that they were woken by an unsmooth breath or the way the flat sheet of a bed stirs when another breathes or the way the throat almost coughs when the dream nearly wakes. Whimpering. Crying. The children saying the mother's name. The way they said her name was a bell whose cord was wrapped around her throat. Her throat had a heart that beat inside it. If she didn't obey, she was choked.

The mothers had gone so long without seeing stars that they imagined the long-tailed bear in their bedrooms with the sleepy brother pointing toward the hunter and the small ladle leaning nearby. The mothers had gone so long without natural light that their bones began to soften and their clothes began to smell of eucalyptus and their eyes began to read text in the fingerprints smeared along the pane. The mothers clustered together, though they were alone. The plants around them wilted. Dishes grew mold in the sink. When the fruit flies began to swarm the kitchen and sugar ants came in through invisible cracks at the edge of the stove, the mothers took the children upstairs, away from the honeybees that came down the chimney and away from the rainwater stagnating in the pockets of the canopy on the deck, so that they were ready for floods or locusts, though it was only fire ants digging and chewing out beneath the weed-filled whiskey barrel. Only the turkey chicks feeding on the grass seed tossed at each bare patch.

There were mothers leaning in the supermarkets and mothers panicking in the convenience stores and mothers taking toddlers by the wrists in the gift shops with the fragile figurines. On the mantel, pictures of the mothers though their faces faded from day to day and their chemistries could not refix such ink. The mothers' shoes collected cobwebs in the corners and their coats hung until the shoulders wrinkled in a permanent wave. The sleeves drooped and grew used to being empty. The pockets filled with soot.

The mothers grew allergic to the saliva of dogs and sneezed and whimpered as it was carried through the house by shed fur and air currents. The mothers wove baskets from the limp and dirty dish towels and old books on their shelves. Small rain boots filled the corners. Headless dolls covered the floors.

Rains came and the children became the sound of falling water. Snows came and the children became the way the breath can be seen. Every second of sleep seemed like running someplace unfamiliar. Every word pronounced knew a different word by name.

When the mothers grew too weak to say *no* or to say *yes* or to say *brush your teeth* or *put on your clothes* or *don't make me come down there* or *stop* or *what are you doing to me*, they took to their beds. Anyone would have taken to their beds. Most would never have risen again. But the children were climbing on the couch. They could fall. The children were running down the stairs. They could stumble. The children were inhaling great mouthfuls of food. They could choke. The children were pulling each other by the hair the children were too close to the water the children were at the window ledge the children were seeing something they shouldn't they needed to be fed they needed to be fixed they needed their toys adjusted they needed to drink they needed to need they needed to get sick and get well and the fevers were hell and the crowning of teeth and the bedtime refusals and the need to be touched. The mothers. There were no mothers. There were machines.

They inhaled when the lungs loosened. They looked out past all the dead crickets on the screen. They scrubbed on hands and knees the markers that had streaked uncapped across the linoleum floor and the rug where the one shit without a Pull-Up on and the place where the other spilled a full bowl of cereal into the chair and the place where the handprints stayed caked with dirt and the place where one said no and the other said nothing and no one was listening and nothing was done/right/okay/clean/calm.

Every twitch of every muscle. Spasm in the children's bellies. Every episode of vertigo. Every allergy to the milk of the breast.

When they tried to weep, the mothers conjured a dry scrape in the apex of their throats. When they tried to walk away, they came back. When they tried to take a breath, it came out. *Stop. Share. Get off your sister. Get down. Be careful. Stop.*

WHAT TO LEAVE,
WHAT TO UNEARTH

I found out Harry was dead two years after it happened, while look-ing for a picture of him online. What I found was an obituary. He'd always said he'd never do heroin because it would be sure to kill him. And now it had.

I remembered the first time we sat together in Sharon's car, he in the driver's seat and me in the passenger's, stiff and strange and left waiting. How he had turned the key so we could listen to the radio. How the dashboard lit up.

He twiddled his thumbs and pretended to whistle a tune. He turned back to the radio and fiddled with the knob, trying to find a clear station. When only static poured in, he jerked the knobs free of the stereo and threw them out the windows we had cracked so we could smoke.

I knew even then that this was a connection I might start at the end of the world, as buildings fell and sidewalks crumbled, as fissures opened up in the earth and all I knew was undone by some uncontrollable and inevitable force. In some ways, this was exactly what was happening, since my parents were in the process of their savage divorce. Harry would give me something to hold onto from moment to moment, as the moments themselves came to a halt. There was something edgy and uncertain but also real and running as blood that I could take shelter in. The lined flannel shirts he left in the back of my car and the stolen silver bracelet he gave me in a box, and the watch with hands that glowed in the dark so that I could see the minutes pass in his room and know when I had to rise and get back in order to keep my mother from calling the police. I learned to lie and I learned not to care whether the lies were believed. My parents had broken my heart, they had broken the contract, and I felt that they now had no right to tell me what I could and could not do.

On the braver nights, Harry would pull his old truck into the driveway and rev the engine because the horn didn't work and I would hear the low sound like a seismic disturbance from my room and run out before my mother could stop me. When I was with him I gained the ability to care about nothing and take risks. I lived for the nights we would go and sit out by the water at Allen's Harbor or in the parking lot of the Burger King or in the wet grasses and chain link fences of the Exeter fairgrounds, and I was willing to pay the price when I got home, because by then I'd stolen the time and couldn't be stopped. By then, it was too late.

The girl who had always been so straight and narrow, who had worried about grades and done nothing wrong, learned to sit in the passenger seat as he drove her car through the snowy woods too fast and to drink too much and to kiss recklessly and to love recklessly and to go too fast and not panic when the car smashed and not panic when her parents knew and not panic when the police came. And so my heart rate slowed and my life calmed and I learned to turn shallow eyes to a crisis and just look and not feel the world would end, because what was the world once your world was over?

That first night, I remember we sat in silence for a while and he beat his fingers on the steering wheel in time to the music. Then he pulled back and sat looking at me, the faint green light of the dials and indicators steady, his eyes intensely focused, and asked me if I wanted to walk.

I felt like an archaeologist delicately brushing the dust from long-buried bones to see what lay beneath. Using the most precise tools, working so slowly the progress almost didn't exist.

And when he finally kissed me as we topped the ridge, I didn't make him stop.

On Time

A moment is makeshift. It is constructed of sticks and child's glue despite the strong wind. Huff and puff and you can blow it over. Watch it dissipate like dandelion seed. It sinks between the cough and the orchard, the bow and the string. The elbow in time is the part that gives. Milk stilled in the glass. Trains arriving late. One fabric rubbing at another. Scrimshaw holding the memory of the whale surfacing and sounding, scribble of bone.

I remember when I first felt the future might influence the past. I was expecting a letter and thinking of the letter's arrival in the box. Wondering whether it would be there when I returned, lying pale on its side like a market fish, sealed gills still, happy news or sad. Suddenly I felt the way I crossed the street or the route I took could alter its news, what was said inside. That time didn't just happen one way, past to present. That cause and effect were not as linear as we might think. That what I did right now was influencing my mother's childhood. That the way the weather behaved tomorrow would influence the dawn of the earth.

Einstein tells us all time happens at once.

When I try to remember my first conscious moment, I grasp the vague dream of a red mitten in snow. I know it isn't my first awareness, only the first moment my memory has held.

My life of memory began the night I dreamed of the single red mitten in the snow.

I was four years old. The dream was colorful and tangible and soft. Like touching a chimney full of wind. It was like the small moths that rise up from the uncut grass when one walks through it. Like kerchiefs, like dust, like eyes edged in fright, like the miles before the train comes, or headlights gone dim. Like sunlight coming through a lens to set fire to dried-out leaves.

This mitten was the present and the past. I had dropped a single red mitten in the snow that afternoon, while the light was waning, and when I noticed, I pulled on my mother's hand, but it was too late. She was in a hurry and hadn't seen.

So the mitten was left behind.

Because the clouds filled up and the rain came down. Because the drywall went up and the struts went in. Because the threads let loose and the seams unraveled. Because even houses are filled with wolves.

When I woke from the dream, I felt a serious dread. An understanding that the world in my mind was dead, but that the world itself was very alive. I had made something in my mind; it wasn't memory, and it also was. All the wormholes opened. All the realities and their shadowy fictions clashed. I understood that I could never truly understand what was real.

I understood the past. I understood the self. I understood that the two were separate, and the same. I was dreaming something in a dream that wasn't real. But I could go outside and the reality would be made. The mitten could be there.

The sensation mimicked the one I felt when I went to the house where I'd grown up. The house was there, and was real. There were trees outside. There was a road out front. But inside the sleeve of that house, inside the tunnel of my seeing that house in my mind, there was the other house, still white with blue shutters, still with a pine tree at the corner that was small. Still with two children playing by digging holes and pretending to cook in them pine cones and stones.

Too much lushness: I couldn't make myself drive past. Everything had grown out of control. The oak at the corner cut back from the telephone wires, the neighbors' bushes along their suspension wall. The pine tree my sister had planted as a sapling towered taller than the roof. Its shadow fell along the length of the house. The room at the corner that had been mine I imagined no longer filled with sun.

It was there beneath the skin of what I was actually seeing, this other skin, the neighborhood of the past. This surface neighborhood was a stranger. That deeper ancient neighborhood was in my very blood. The place where I'd turned off the road to walk the path to elementary school, the sign once sprayed with graffiti, the kind neighbors who knew me, all grown old. The pain of that. Of loss.

The sensation that came with those two houses dividing. Again, the red mitten in my dream, and also outside in the snow.

Maybe it wasn't a dream, but a memory so vague, so far at the beginnings of memory, that it seemed like one.

When I carried my children, I remember reading they could dream in the womb. I remember looking at my daughter during the ultrasound, as she sat curled at the bottom, a long way down, gazing straight up, seemingly at me. I remember the camera traveling my son's spine until it looked like the backbone of a dragon or a fish. I remember holding him as a sleeping newborn in the hospital as he twitched, as his eyes paced the rooms beneath their lids, back and forth, and feeling excluded. He'd known me such a short time. A dream. He was inside himself. I wasn't there, and I doubted he could remember me; I was so new. Then suddenly his lips puckered and his mouth suckled, and I was overjoyed. I was there! He was dreaming of eating. And so dreaming of me.

I was in that moment aware: I was my son's past, his present, his future. I had grown his teeth and eyelashes and fingernails and wrist bones in my body, with the material of my body. Someplace, cells of his still floated in me. He had made me a chimera. His cells were in my body. His cells were in my brain.

When Einstein dreamed of the universe's shape, he dreamed differences added in velocities, at 186,000 miles per second: light speed. The moving beam versus the moving ball. He was dreaming of people aging more slowly on spaceships shaped like whales and traveling at the speed of light. He dreamed of density, hyperbolic curvatures, flatnesses and spheres. He dreamed of an infinity. Sheets of paper and leather saddles, tidied bedspreads and empty shoeboxes. Collapsing. He dreamed existence as the skin of a balloon, spinning teacups and fireworks and tailspins of stars.

Traveling quickly, we age more slowly. Even in cars. Even on trains. We may travel more quickly in space, but any forward accelerated movement means the slowing of age. How is this possible? Don't we age by years? Don't we age by moments strung together in a necklace of our memories and developments and scars? Time is elastic, is relative. And, for us, is largely dictated by memory.

But my brain at times also remembers the future. I know someone will call. And they do. I know I will see someone I haven't seen for years at an event, am *sure* of it, and they are there. I know six deer will appear in the road. The six deer appear.

Déjà vus occur that are so powerful, I know what will be said next. I follow a conversation I already remember. Perhaps an as-yet-unpractical or unused part of the brain contains a memory of the future. Perhaps our descendants will see all time at once, and cause and effect will move forward instead of back.

Right before it happened, I dreamed of my grandfather's death. It was the day after my grandmother died. In the dream, my grandfather sat on the passenger side of a gray wagon. It was hitched to a gray horse, in a gray room. The reins draped lax in the driver's seat. I went around to the back of the wagon, where a gray mirror hung on the gray wall. When I looked in the mirror, I saw my dead grandmother's face. Then I got up on the bench beside my grandfather, took the reins in my hands, and drove the wagon off.

A week later, I got the call: my grandfather had been struck by a car while crossing at the crosswalk on Eighty-Sixth Street in Brooklyn, four blocks from their apartment.

Three days after that, I found myself saying goodbye to him as he lay unconscious in a hospital bed. Never before had I seen stubble on his chin. When I wasn't watching him, I watched the East River barges move like the slow bodies of those who have come to witness the last days of one they love.

The moment is a drop about to fall from a leaf, a floor about to be swept, an empty parking lot at dawn, seashore-white. The moment is water from a faucet poured into a cup.

I can't tell you how because there is no how. Or maybe there are too many. An orb weaver builds a web in the corner of my daughter's room, lays eggs there, comes down from the ceiling on a long strand. I examine the web, the places the strands intersect, shapes made and contained. In the scaffolding, strands that aren't there but also make the web: air, atom, molecule, nucleus, material from an exploded star, black hole pull, the spider's last meal, the creation of webbing in her spinnerets.

I examine the abdomen of the spider, hourglass shape, nautilus shape, cactus shape, iris shatter, galaxy splay. Fragment and fractal. Einstein's universe there. Time there, future and past. A language there, an obelisk of hieroglyphs, spinning words not quite understood, as though they were whispered just below the threshold of the ear's ability to hear.

My daughter dreamed this spider while still in the womb. My daughter dreamed it there in the time before she could remember, until it was real. There in her brain, the contours and movements, the intricacies, angles, and absences, the legs, the hourglass abdomen, the fractals and webs of her synapses firing, the darkness before and after it exists.

THE MECHANICS

B egin.

The heart agitates its repetitive combustions and compressions. The breath's blind rodent tunnels branch-like depths. Brainwaves shake off their sleep spindles and K complexes, grow asynchronous and frequent.

Perceive stimuli. Establish context. Wake.

Only then are the restless and greedy excursions of the crows heard, or the chill which seals the pores and pinches up the arm's fine hairs felt. Only then do the eyes open to the initial foggy prospect of light. Images curve as if inside a spoon. Rods fox the cones. Only then do the tendons hoist their sails.

Predict the future. Recreate the past. Even before the pupil has time to contract.

Last night, I slept deeply. I had a whiskey sour. I sat out on the deck and watched puddles hallucinate the auras of wind. The water left its damp in the soles of my shoes.

Once these territories are secured, once the self has grown sure, let the lashes flex and glaze, let the iris swim in its feathered froth and ruddy smolder like a jellyfish loose in its own poisoned frays. Kick-start the action's grand arc.

Pull the great whale of the body from its animal waters.

Throw the light switch: a mousetrap springs. Electricity halved is mended by way of metal. It travels the filament in a bright incision.

When called on by the well pump, water comes to snake through this husk of wood, the house. Felled trees the lumberjack took and dragged from the forest with calipers and hooks. Those irons of the earth molded to nails. Those rough hands laying shingles made from the black liquid compacted from long-dead animals preserving in the earth. Poured to the porcelain bowl and the molding that holds it in place. Drained to the elbow pipe that leads to the septic system and leech field, that bit of green, infiltrated grass.

The stairs: minor drops and a stiff spine along the wall to cling to. Lift the feet and let them go. The thighs contract and release like pistons, with the quiver of a series of pulleys or springs.

Soon you will walk to the door. The pins of hinges will spin flawlessly in place, their tumblers aligned like the milk teeth of your pocket's jagged key. Hungry edges gritting their grind on the pocket's lining and snagging at the threads and chewing with each step at a different tidy stitch.

You will walk to your car, ignite, ignite, one foot on the gas and a hop of light and breath will spark and the gas will go up in flames and a great roar as all the tiny segments conduct one another through mechanical motions that mimic the heart. Turn the crankshaft. Turn the fan belt. Inject the gas. The slow center of the wheel turns like a galaxy center spinning with a twist of stars and the hubcap upends and then goes unseen and you are for the traveling, the road's single pebbles blur and you are gone.

You will navigate streets where bitumen is poured each spring to mend the frost heaves and where the roots of trees wrestle with the sidewalks and win. Right at the high school. Left at the bank. Straight through the stoplight. Just above you, the past wavers; objects are closer than they appear. Through the blue tint, you ride and veer. Your brakes give off particles of asbestos.

You will go to, leave from. You will assassinate the character you have been each moment, shedding skin, losing memories, time slowing or speeding up or not real and just perception. Cause and event, nothing separate from that. You will make a new seeing through your dreams and through the search for remedies in what all this being means.

Meanwhile, unseen flora covers your skin. Stars die. Planets spin and fail to break free of their orbits. Stars go dark after they go large. A universe expands. If Einstein is right about the way time happens, you will live and die and live again. These lives will be labyrinths you wander with one shoulder to the wall.

KNOCK WOOD

When I broke my finger and they grafted in the dead person's bone, it almost killed me. My lips swelled and so did the inside of my throat. My nostrils swelled shut while I slept. The inside of my mouth blew up. I would wake to the realization that I wasn't breathing. Panic was a new form of bedroom dark. Twice I woke to the knowledge that my throat was closed completely, and I knew I would die. But it opened again once I sat up.

They put me on prednisone without telling me it would make me more afraid than I already was. Prednisone and antihistamines and Zantac and an EpiPen. I didn't want to sleep but I had to sleep. I kept my daughter in the bed with me because she made me feel secure. Or made me feel motherly. I wasn't sure which. I would sit and tremble in the bedside chair, trying to convince myself I didn't need to go to the hospital. I went to the emergency room five times, until the co-payments became too much to afford. Then I would drive there and sit in the car outside until I felt it was okay to go home.

My husband thought I was making it all up. He would sit on the side of the bed while I panicked and wait to be allowed to go back to sleep. He wanted everything to be okay. He wanted me to be fine. This continued for three months. I finally got up the courage to tell him I was afraid of dying, one morning in the bathroom while the children slept, and he told me I needed help. Years later he told me he'd thought I was just having panic attacks until I was diagnosed.

The first time I saw Tim, I knew he was the cure. His form of trouble was a distraction from death. Like a bit of inflammation in the body at all times. But an inflammation of the mind and heart, something to keep it busy. The day I met him, I had been working to quell my panic because the stress caused by my fear of the swelling would cause me to swell. That night I went to an event with round tables and drinks, and when I saw him, I knew two things: that he didn't like anyone, and that I wanted to make him like me.

Of course he was wearing black. A jacket and shirt and jeans. The way he looked at me made me afraid. His gaze had a boring in, like he would not leave any part of me for myself. He wanted to see me. In ways that seeing couldn't see. So he started talking. And I started talking. Until we could see each other whole through the talking, an ocean, a wake, a surface beneath which we understood there was more and more. We turned each other inside out. We were mollusks with the softness of organs for a shell. We kept talking in order to uncover an underneath. We started talking, and we haven't stopped since.

Once he told me he'd had a vision, or a form of vision, while in an open square in Bath. He'd stood between buildings while seagulls flew up, calling and screaming, headed for the sea. Wheeling. White. He said in that moment he realized how many moments were passing while we were apart, parallel moments, moments we should share. Countless moments, like the cobblestones there. I thought this was ironic, given that moment in Seattle when the seagulls had seemed to be my whole life flying up, my choice vanishing like smoke. But these were seagulls counted in the flesh, each of their bodies another minute lost.

The next time we were together, he gave me a pocket watch as a gift. It was sterling silver with ornate engravings, swirlings and scrolls. Maybe one continuous line. When I clicked it open, I saw the words inscribed inside: *toi seulement*. Then I saw the second hand jerking and halting. Military leg marching. Arm kept stiff against the body. War against our time with each other, against our being together. Since moments happened in the flesh, and I could never be two places at once.

Then we went to the museum and stumbled across the painting of the two sinners turning their backs on God, and we knew the dark wild surrounding the figures was our own. We returned to it over and over on different trips to the same city, sometimes meandering to it through other rooms, sometimes running as the guards yelled behind us that the museum was about to close. Before it, he gave me his dead mother's wedding ring, the one that had been lost by her once and then found seven years later when she looked out the kitchen window and saw a gleam in the garden, a gleam in the dirt. It was a tiny ring. We were shocked when it fit.

Slowly, my swelling subsided. Slowly, my throat began to open up. Slowly, I began to live without always fearing I would die.

Years after the discovery of the painting, I took my children to the same museum, but all I could see was the shade beneath the tree cast on that stretch of unoccupied sidewalk where the tuba had appeared. Where we had walked behind it holding hands. I could feel us walking together, but in reality I was showing my children the mummies of ancient Egypt and the vases of ancient Greece. I saw the ghosts of us there where we always were, because we always were everywhere we had once been. Our footsteps happening in time, our happiness in the sun.

Then a day happened: an anniversary. Anniversary of the day I had taken the train to New York, anniversary of three days before Harry's death. Anniversary of no-turning-back. It was all coincidence—reschedulings, long waits, limited availabilities—that created the convergences. My husband was tested for Asperger's Syndrome, was soon to be diagnosed. Tim's divorce was declared final. My mother and I went to see a therapist. My son played in a baseball game that happened beneath a gathering storm. All these convergences—my husband telling the sheet of paper he had no feelings, Tim snapping a lasting bond, me digging deep into the horrific past, a storm lifting and the dark clouds turning rose-colored—made me realize there could be no end to the tunnel. There could be no outcome. There could be no end. Every moment was the bat hitting the ball. Every moment had the undersides of leaves blowing to exposure in a way that predicted rain. This was a ride that had run out of our control. It was a series of threads woven together by something larger than ourselves. It would use us up. It would kill us if it could.

The storm of that day came the next day instead. It blew the plants off the railings and chairs from the deck, and the cats hid and those crows already airborne were tossed. Insects burrowed into tunnels of decayed trees and the turkeys went deeper into the woods. The mourning doves were silent. The air felt heavy, like closely woven wool. Disquieting, like Tim's delayed appearance at the train station, once I breathed it in. Then I knew what would happen. Nothing would kill us after all. We were the unruly ones. We were the gluttons. We were the ones who had torn open a hole in the order of the world. The end would sob instead of scream. The end would whisper instead of rage. It would happen so naturally, it would be as though we chose it, as though we killed ourselves.

WHY I BECAME A CRIMINAL

So how do you tell it. To someone who doesn't know. To someone who's never felt the rush. The chill. The risk. The promise. To someone who's never left the path for the woods. Who's never fished down at the creek. Who's never felt the blood rise and the eyes lead to a place that tastes like gold. How do you tell it. It goes so deep down it isn't a place. It is cicadas at dusk. It is the rush of steam from the manhole cover. It is the leak of filth from the gutter, the travel of the leaf's husk along the rake of the muddy waters. It has the hiss of a snake. It has the breakdown of an unloved daughter.

How do you tell it. It is old like books but without the molder. It is clean like soap but without the scent. It sends a rush out behind it like a ferry as it turns to dock within the spine's lace. How do you compare it. When all is lost. It has the mapping out of an antique print, that razor's edge of black and white. It defies time. It sees you as the enemy. How does it know what you think, what you want. It has the haunt of old houses with their creaks and their swollen steps and their pantries filled with potatoes left so long they turn to dark liquid or grow long, skeletal eyes. Gun in the hand. Knife at the throat. Headlights off. Breath smelling of whiskey and smoke. Teardrop-shaped moments lengthening until they can no longer hang and drop into the quiet of a well so far down, into the winter at the palm of your hand.

How can you tell it. The paint dries. The clotheslines fray. The cottages fill with spiders. The marshes cry with flawless pearls of birds, like piano keys: a little pressure and they fly off and the air is disturbed by the frequencies of ghosts. How to tell it. There must be a way. There is a man beside you, or a woman, and they lean in close and you know what is going to happen next, and there you are at the scene with all the longing intact. It takes you to the goose-bumping of flesh. It takes you to a season of rain. It takes you to roots and takes you to rivals and takes you to the very blood boiling in the pan and takes you to the window-shatter of what you ask as you speed it up, as you dig it down, as you crown it king, as it lingers with the ways you behave.

What is it what is it, why can't you set it down, get it collared, get it ploughed, why can't you get it under wraps. It has seen what you are, what they do, where I am, and it will not ask again. It is what rules you even when you think you can make your own choices. There is no clean. There are only the demons it knows to set free. There are only the noises it knows to mimic and the newspapers it knows not to read. There are photographs of scenes that have never existed. There are twists in a rope that has never been twisted. There are clip-offs in a cliff face and a freefall you never meant that can break a femur and bloody a lip and a wisp of milkweed that brushes your cheek and there is the way you put your chin into the wind so as to feel the direction of the earth as it spins. You are standing on the graves of men, you are standing with your hand on your hip and one foot slightly offset, you are apart, you are aware. You are there and you are not.

And should you begin to run to be one with the cactus grass, should you begin to part with weeds and scatter the drying clover and scintillate the wind, should you begin and gather speed, a gradual rhythm to render the energy kinetic, what you feel and what you think will translate into this and you will remember the moment the police came and you went for the woods and the blue lights made the trees a strobe of neon as you fled and you could feel the others fleeing around you. Like water. Like mice. Being parted by the trees, being scratched in the face, pants torn at the knees, coming to the guard rail and leaping, coming to the old piles of stones, coming to a place that opened onto a field in the dark but for the moon, and there were only a few of them but many of us and you could feel their breath and tender the currency of their battery lights like tiny echoes of an elegant star. And you could feel them then: they were the past in your blood, the racket it makes and its tiny hands branching like a sea fan or crinolined tissue or crumple of dusk. There is nothing to tell, there is little to remember. It is like a life you haven't lived or a lens you haven't matched to your eye. The blur is there, it has your heartbeat slowing, it has the other leaning in in the green of the dashboard light, it has the radio playing a forgotten song that recalls an old bar in another broken town. It has it all.

How do you tell it. There is nothing to tell. There was no one there. The moment was pure, it struck like lightning, you were only its tool as it journeyed to the ground and then you were left significant and empty and you had a feel like so little was lost. But it all was lost and you picked yourself up and the world kicked into gear, you went right on, you had no choice, there was nothing to lose but the good of the earth, that scent of something new, that feel of being alive as if, as if. But there is no if, not now, not then, so go and end. There is nothing to be done.

You lost the men who ran in pursuit. Next time you would end up in the tiny painted room with the names carved again and again into the wood of the bench, and someone possibly watching through the two-way mirror, without shoes, without a belt. You would sit and feel your life crashing down and its ruin eating through you, until you stepped out with a court date or fine or strong lecture about the friends you choose and the streets infected you again with their momentum and their reckless knowledge that this life will fade. The root is despair, the root is the cut that rivets your heart. There is no healing, there is no cure, nothing is certain. The allure of the wreck and the shout are too strong, and the broken beer bottle and the thrown fist and the stolen car and the one-way street, the allure of speed and chance to throw the die. But better to spill the liquor of what happens at night, to go there and then go further, to be aware and then be dumber, to love the thick cascade of strangers' tongues and the feel as the truck wheels let the angle go, to wonder if the cab will turn over and you will be found come morning under the powerlines or along the salty shore or under the stage of the bandstand or in the playground dirt. To stumble drunk and know you can spit insults and drive crazy and blame the beer. To be found there near the junkyard or the scrap metal, near the quarry or the military base, all those places abandoned at night where the brick walls rise and the shadows hull like boats.

To be found there or not to get out or not to be caught or not to be jailed or not to stand at the pay phone in the night and tell your mother you will be home though you will not be home. How to say it. There is no reason. There is no time when you are there and the long roads through the empty storefronts are aging and the dropouts are gathering in the shadowy lens of a nearby convenience store and the parents are drinking their cheap wine.

I can't tell you. I can't let you in. This town has its very own secrets. Go there. See for yourself. You can see it if you sit for a long time and listen. Underneath each place is a nighttime of abandon. The reckless hour. The old moans of the children raised by a soft despair still singing. Listen for yourself. The neighborhoods will tell you. The man on his front porch with a gun in his hands. The children playing in the streets. A cocked rifle says this. A police-issue baton in your face. Go from the rooms out to the streets. They will remember you. They will reinterpret your tidy name. They will leach you of your hope and teach you to pass on the narrow bridge with your headlights turned off while kissing the person in the passenger seat. You might live through it. And that would be worse. Its curse will sit in your breast until you die. You will long for something else. You will sing the hymns of savages. Your only church will be yourself, church of the sin, church of the rush, church of the film on the unwashed windows along the busiest street. Church of response to all of this, a wish. Church of need and not-have and want.

Latent Print

When we arrived at the address the dispatcher had given, the man was standing out on his front porch in the January dark, soaking wet, trembling in a short sleeved V-neck undershirt, his breath rising up, his hair drenched. He was holding what looked like a pot of boiled potatoes; they were steaming in the cold. He had a fork poised in his hand. When we pulled into the driveway, he didn't look up.

The call said that a house had flooded, and as soon as we entered the apartment, we saw that several inches of water covered the floor. The power was out. I stood at the edge of the deluge, a mere prosecutor's office intern, as the officers put on their flashlights and the strong beams illuminated glimpses of the rooms. There didn't seem to be much furniture. Someone said, *The plumbing's been pulled from the dishwasher. See these hoses? They go under here.*

Then I heard them asking the man what had happened. He didn't answer. He kept his head down and held tight to the handle of the pot.

The carpet was sopping wet and I could feel my feet sink in, as if I were walking across a just-used kitchen sponge. It was too dark to see anything except for the circling flashes of the aimed beams and the silhouette of the figure, his pants and bedraggled hair and bony wrists, and the glow off the potatoes swollen and blanched in their skins. The voices of the two officers sounded far off, like organ notes heard from outside a church. The open door was letting flakes of snow drift in.

As I looked at this man, standing with his jeans drenched almost to the knee in a home that he had flooded himself, I remembered what had happened the day my mother and I pulled up to an inter- section at a red light in Staten Island. As we sat waiting, I became aware of a homeless man hovering on the island between us and the oncoming traffic. I didn't turn for fear of drawing his attention, but examined him from the corner of my eye. He was just a few paces away, and I could see a ragged dark blue sweatshirt with the hood pulled up, torn corduroys, damaged sneakers, and shoulders that stooped as he dragged on his cigarette. I checked to be sure the doors were locked.

As the crosswalk light changed to green, the man started to cross in front of the car, and something about the way he moved suddenly seemed familiar. The loose gait. The crooked fingers clutching the cigarette. I couldn't see his face under the sweatshirt hood, but there was something I couldn't quite deny there.

Then it clicked. The man was my uncle. My father's brother. My Uncle Al.

How long had it been since I'd seen him? Ten years? Fifteen? He would know me, since he had known me since I was born, but what would happen if I were to appear, a stranger off the street running to grab his arm, a stranger coming out of a car calling his name? He was bipolar manic depressive. Paranoid schizophrenic. *Would* he know me? And yet it didn't seem right to not acknowledge him, to ignore the fact that he was there. He was *family*. How could I just drive off?

By the time he had reached the far side of the street, I could see the bottom half of his face and the rim of his glasses, and I was certain it was him. He turned onto the sidewalk to continue on his way, smoking his cigarette, stooped. Then the light changed. I felt the car moving forward. My mother was beginning to drive away and I hadn't said a word. I realized then that we were on Father Capodanno Boulevard, just down the street from the New Broadview Manor, the halfway house where my uncle lived. He was my own blood, a family member I hadn't seen in years, and I had failed to acknowledge him, had let him just walk away.

This man, in his flooded apartment, reminded me of my uncle. He gave off a similar air, of disturbance, of insanity, sitting on the floor now just inside the open door. The officers were preparing to leave; I could hear it in the tone of their voices.

As I moved to follow them, the headlights of a passing car hit the living room window and I saw smears across the glass. The panes were covered with the streaks of the man's hands, with figures and shapes that looked like hieroglyphs, fingerprints and letters and sketches. It was clear that he had been writing there for months, for as I turned I saw that all the windows were covered. I was in a cathedral of the skin's oils, of the finger's singular prints and whorls. It was the language of my father's brother, a language the officers were deaf to, a language I couldn't quite hear.

Perhaps he had written an SOS to his long-gone mother. Perhaps he had scrawled out his name. And yet no one would understand, not me, not the social worker I was sure would come, whom I knew the officers had already phoned. All the scribbling would be erased by her when she arrived, or by the landlord once the man was taken away—all the transmissions undone, all the letters left undelivered, all the filth washed clean.

PROCEDURES FOR AN OUTING

If you are to take Kathy and Al to lunch, you must take them someplace familiar. A place they know, the Burger King within walking distance or the run-down diner at the neighborhood's edge.

You must remember Al's hat. Any of his hats. They give him the ability to hide in public. The brim allows him to duck down and away when the room full of strangers seems too much.

If Kathy gets upset, she will raise her voice.

If Kathy gets euphoric, she will raise her voice.

In both of these situations, if you cannot calm her down, expect that you will have to leave to keep from causing a scene.

Al must be able to smoke. He can go outside to do so, but be sure he brings his cigarettes. You know from his brown fingers that he is perpetually smoking. Ignore Al's brown fingers. Ignore his yellowed teeth.

In order to avoid guilt, do not look at the state of their clothing. Do not see the hole in the elbow of Al's sweatshirt or the ragged threadbare legs of his jeans. Do not see that Kathy is wearing a shirt that is a size too small and used to have a bow or button at the neck. When Kathy pulls her glasses from her bag to read the menu, do not notice that the left arm is missing from the frames. Ignore the way they tilt on her face.

Do not notice her missing teeth, the yawning black gaps at the back of her mouth.

Kathy will sigh. She will exclaim. She will say over and over again how happy she is to see you.

Al will move constantly as if his nerves are on strings, his loose limbs shrugging and fingers twitching, his knees jiggling to an unheard song, his thighs swinging wide and then jostling back. Pretend not to notice.

When Al says, *My brain's just not right today,* pretend you didn't hear.

Keep it level. Keep the conversation clean. Do not address _____ (this will be plural).

Remember how beautiful Kathy once was, as she sits in her floral shirt designed for the obesely overweight, her fingers strangled by rings that once fit, her breath heavy, her yellow fingernails scratching at her neck.

Remember the time you slept on your grandmother's living room couch and Kathy stayed up all night, stubbing out cigarettes in the overfilled ashtrays on the kitchen table, calling the operator to ask the time, talking to herself about things that hadn't happened, moving in and out of the fluorescent overhead light.

Remember Al coming into that kitchen with the radio to his ear. His hair greasy and his glasses smeared. The threat of violence as he said, *Don't you shout at me* or *Ma, you need to get the hell out.* The time your mother guided you out to the car by your shoulder. How your grandmother called them "bad days," as in, *Alfred is having a bad day.*

Remember how no one got them help.

When Kathy starts a sentence with *I remember* or *I miss* or *I wish* or a lengthened *Oh,* ask her if she needs another napkin or if you can get her anything else to eat.

If Kathy is so medicated that she sits and stares and doesn't seem to understand what is happening when you say her name, take your time eating and relax.

When Al starts to mumble to himself under his breath, ask for the check.

Tip well. Smile at the waitress. Attempt a gracious exit. Do not make eye contact with the other diners as you move towards the door. Do not wait for the leftovers to be packed up. Do not order dessert.

INVASIVE SPECIES

I don't want to remember. Memory is that bush in the yard that we keep cutting down as it keeps growing back. I don't know what species it is. It is the kind that has berries you can't eat. Bird berries, my mother used to call them. Red and round and smooth. Now I tell my daughter, *Don't eat them. They'll make you sick.*

The fruit of memory: it makes you sick. You cut it flush with the ground and maybe burn where it has been. But slowly its stray, disordered branches clamor up and leaves form and even before you realize it has begun to grow, it's a bush again. Casting shadows. Blocking your way down some narrow path. Dominating the subtle slope that your yard takes on, the one that makes it good for sledding in winter. It will take over. It may grow thorns. It will govern in many directions at once. Each of those red berries a point of focus, a droplet of blood.

If I'm lucky, the past is instead a bracelet with a broken clasp, resting slackly on the wrist. Soon to fall loose and be lost.

DEAD RECKONING

Something in me knew all along that I should get out while I could.

I spent all of July and August playing pool, sneaking out, smoking pot. Wearing his heavy flannel shirt when it got cold. Listening as he told me he didn't care if he ended up in jail because he'd done all he wanted to do. Kissing while he tried to pass other cars on the frighteningly narrow Jamestown Bridge. I loved the way he called me Mario. The way he called me Skid.

We broke up the night I caught him at a friend's house with another girl. But I continued to see Harry behind his new girlfriend's back, to park at the old sawmill and kiss him in the wide backseat, while he continued to spend Saturday nights in a home unsupervised by parents and continued to con his way out of any crime for which he was caught. He worked as a dishwasher at a local restaurant until he was fired for stealing food. He stole a car when someone left it running at a gas station while they went inside to pay. He drove it all the way to the southern part of the state before a cop recognized the make and model and called it in.

Finally, I did the only thing I could. I started dating his friend Joe as a cowardly form of revenge.

The night of the party in the woods, Harry appeared suddenly out of the dark. He took my hand and led me off while Joe was busy getting another beer. We sat down in a spot at the top of a hill where the trees sheltered us from sight and he started kissing me without a word. I knew I should stop him, but at the same time I felt my heart pounding. It'd been over a year since I'd seen him. I'd missed him.

After a while, Harry pulled away and lay down with his hands behind his head. His face was barely visible. He looked out over the dark trees and down to where we could just see the glow of the bonfire beyond the brush and slope. Then he said suddenly, "I'm an alcoholic, Jen."

I realized that the slight tang I had tasted behind his tongue had the acidity of vomit.

I reached out to touch his face. He laughed and rolled away from me, down the hillside, and lay there prone and still on the open face of the slope. I followed, crawling down on my hands and knees, brushed back the hair from his face, and leaned down to kiss him.

Then I heard a shout rise up from behind me, and I jerked my head up. There was Joe running at us, yelling, pulling Harry roughly to his feet. He hit him again and again, in the face, in the gut. I realized our roll down the hill had made us visible to everyone at the party. It all happened so quickly that Harry had no time to react; he was limp in Joe's grasp, holding his arms over his head like a child.

Almost as soon as I realized it was happening, the scuffle between the two of them was interrupted by someone who had been standing to one side. I saw Joe get hit so hard that he fell down, like a sack of dry concrete thrown in the bed of a truck.

I pushed up on my hands, shoving against the ground on either side of my body, stumbled once, and rose. The boys fought their way down the hill and disappeared into the woods. I ran after them, but then there were cars pulling out and someone said the police were coming. In the chaos, I knew there was no chance I would find them. But I was Joe's ride. How would he get home?

I managed to stumble to my car, parked in a clearing among the others. I pulled out and raced down the dark roads, unsure of where I was going, whispering under my breath. I half expected to see Joe walking by the side of the road or to glimpse his body in a ditch. It was my fault. I wondered whether he was alive. I felt a loyalty that surprised me. I was shocked to feel a stir that had nothing to do with Harry. I had the ability to hurt Joe. And he was willing to fight for me.

When I got to the corner Mobil station, our hangout and meeting spot, I saw a giant of a boy I recognized emerging from the convenience store. I realized this was the shape I had seen in the woods, the one who had interrupted the fight and defended Harry. I pulled in and ran up to him, breathless.

"Where's Joe?" I asked.

He looked down at his shirt and, with both hands, pulled it out from his body to show something to me. The shirt was dark with wetness, the entire front of it, in a broad stain spread across the belly and chest and creeping up onto the arms. It was soaked with red, I realized. It was covered with blood.

"Here's Joe," he said. Then he laughed.

KNOCK WOOD

In spring, Tim and I crossed the Thames to lie beneath a cherry tree planted in the shadow of Saint Paul's dome. Past the man selling chestnuts in the plaza, past the crosswalk where the traffic lights changed. There was a square of loam around it and we lay looking up into its clouds, the pink petals fretting when the wind blew, dark branches threading through like the bronchioli of lungs. The sounds of cars passing drifted from the nearby road, people glanced down as they walked. But we were in a secret cupola made of finery and lilt. Spun glass. Snow and blood. Looking up. Sun in our eyes. Beyond it, the steady presence of the cathedral. Beyond it, the mindlessness of sky.

This tree was unlike the trees that had grown outside my grandparents' house. Those trees like moths caught between the window and the screen. Those trees that had the look of a dog begging to be let inside. Those trees that split concrete the way events split the mind. With roots using slow time to work their way back up. At night, I would imagine them just outside, growing through the sidewalks, breaking the city in half. I imagined them making a low sound as if they had throats, though the sound was the sound of the cement giving, the layers people once alive had laid down to defeat nature and so to defeat death. But I could hear an opening from below, the ill tree finding a way to stretch, the slabs buckling, their gross crumble, the water mains compromised, the manhole covers manipulated and lifted, even the smallest sapling finding its way in the little soil and dust.

The metropolis had worked for so long to lay those tidy blocks side by side, to make order, to construct, to align, but the roots had come strong and wild from the dirt.

The roots of this cherry tree twined farther somehow, into my mind, into the chambers of my heart. I could feel it like a vine at my rib cage, slowly cracking me apart. Once, I saw a tombstone grown half into a trunk. As the tree widened, it had engulfed the stone, taken it over, so that half the name of the person buried was unreadable. The lip of the wood sealed against the old granite. Someday the whole of the stone would be gone inside the body of the tree.

The roots cracked open the way I saw and felt, found where I would hide and picked apart bit by bit the stark line I would walk. They saw the superstitions, that I avoided the sidewalk cracks, that I knocked on wood. And there was my animal self staring me in the face, until I remembered the deer shot by hunters in Vermont. I was three years old when I stayed at the farmhouse and saw the carcasses hung by their hind legs from every barn. The eyes empty. The bodies cut open and the organs taken out.

I was open now. The tree took my sense of one moment following the next. It took my ability to balance. Its roots tripped me up. I could imagine my brain as a trellis and when the vine had gone far enough there would be a season when it would flower and I would be gone for good among the pleasant-smelling trumpets and red explosions.

The tree was bright. It had the luster of my grandmother's rare laugh ringing like a toast between two half-filled glasses. It had the tint of my manic aunt's pills, snow globes that showed things dissolving, snow globes of houses crumbling and splintered trees and snow made of paper that once was the sky. It had their undoing of moments, their destruction of the senses, their seizure of time. It was a pact with the starved moon, a pact with the absence, a pact where love prevails.

I would suffocate here. I would be undone slowly, lace by lace, and in place of me the solid wood, the heartwood, the sap, in place of me the insect nests and larvae and hives. In place of me, the muted sound of birdsong. The woodpecker's call. One forgets the self after a time. Until all one has is the long sense of having lived and the depth, like water, of a sigh.

I remembered that at that same graveyard, on a fresher grave, someone had placed a plastic Christmas tree decorated with tiny strung ornaments. A sleigh. A candy cane. A clock.

I would be gone. My name engulfed. Any mark that I had ever existed erased. Inside the tree, I would be in a dark that couldn't breathe and I would wish my way out, a nymph, but with no hope for a magic spell or kiss because this was the real world of cells and structures and organs and weeds, where everything could be explained. I would remain trapped in its tower for thousands of years.

When we rose, the back of Tim's coat was covered in petals. There were petals in my hair. We were getting into a taxi. We were going to see a friend. Everywhere we went, we would leave a trail of petals behind.

Petals numberless like the increments of our exchange. Tim tried to keep track. How many emails, how many photographs, how many hours on Skype. Until it all became too much. Until an infinity passed through and consumed it. Our time together limited but also forever, so many words and images and expressions and memories. Growing and growing. Branching interminably out.

He filmed us as we were lying there. The cherry blossoms in clusters. Our faces close up, passing in and out of the frame. My mouth. His eye. An ear. There was a joy in my face that I didn't know could exist. Tim says, *How much do you love me?* I look at him. I smile. My hand appears. The frame tilts. I hear my voice. *Hi, us in the future.*

THE LIVING ROOM

There were things about my grandparents' house that I feared. In the living room, the chiming clock grinding something sluggish out over the room, the pendulum swing, calculated, controlled. The slow tick, the sluggish tock, the clock's voice like a sermon speaking, like a pastor speaking of sin. Light would change like a remedy tasted but sour, scalding the throat. Time was under its spell, or we were under the spell of time, sitting there in our patent leather shoes with our stockinged knees together, with our hands folded in our laps. Voices silent. Backs straight.

The *tock tock* was a cluck of disdain. It was the click to a horse. The hand coming down: *tock tock*. It was the swing of each of us on the rope over the river. Before the drop. Before the long drop when our limbs stung and our lungs could fill with water. The long surface's meniscus breaking. The clock was the desperation of being in the body. It was the low call of the gulls before they take wing. We, entrapped by its sentiment. *We.* The sound of a web into which we were spun as struggling prey.

The black and red swirl of patterns in the plastic-covered couch. The undone roses in the carpet, the thick plush shag into which our feet sank, into which voices sank and the noises of passing traffic outside. The encyclopedias with their moldering pages and their outdated entries and their breakfront doors locked with a too-small key. The tocks were the bass drum and the requiem voices. The tocks were thunder as it rumbled through. Sidewalks being laid. Concrete being spilled. The masses emigrating over the nearby bridge. Swing to one side, stop. Swing to one side, stop. Gold-plated. Heavy. Numerals marking the constant ring.

There were rubber bands on the door handles. No one used them but there they were, stored up, red, green, dun-colored, for the day they would be needed. Clusters of rubber bands, rows forearm-thick were they to be placed around a wrist. Things wanted to be bound or joined but instead the rubber bands stood as markers, like lines convicts scratch on cell walls to track the days. Nothing was held together. Nothing was wrapped or sealed or glued or welded or screwed. There were no clothespins. There were no paper clips. There were hardly hinges. Nothing was ever given a Band-Aid or tied up with string.

A thin wooden partition folded out from the wall so that the room could be closed off. In the corner, an armchair recliner. The cabinet in which the television was set. Good wood, good, real flesh of trees, stained dark like the room, heavy to lift. Heartwood. Sapwood. One could imagine the tree being felled. The heavy knobs and antennas and channels changed by hand. The carpet with designs like cowlicks or ocean currents or sperm swimming or sound traveling.

The teardrop lamps hardly gave off light. Lit a circle under them with a dull gray-green feeble array. Heavy shades lidded like the fans of widows dropped open. Like widows' fans expanded across the low half of the face. Veiled. Walking in made us think of oil portraits badly painted and the rain on a November afternoon. The room smelled of staleness. Thresholds waning. The room smelled of the wafting dust of carpets and the gaps that happen between the molding and the frames of the doors, of cabinets long closed and mothballs and the dark closets in which forgotten shoes rested and the way wool coats smelled when they were left hanging in the hall, of the deep clay mud of an ocean's shore and of the way burnt things cool, plastics once they are misshapen and destroyed, children's toys beheaded, beds that no one has changed. The urine of domesticated beasts. Hands no longer at play. Churches where the priests have let incense linger, churches where parishioners have forgotten the open books spilling with words so old they grow obsolete, chapters intricate with blight.

The people. As a child, I was afraid of the people. My grandmother stern, thin and diabetic, with her strong mouth and dark coffee hair. Tall and severe. Red lipstick undisturbed. Pasta pot boiling. Table set. Stove fan on. Wiping her hands on a dishcloth. The slight overlap of her front teeth, her hair pulled back from her face. My grandfather adrift in the living room chair, dozing with his mouth open, barely able to speak, stumbling when he walked, stooping, arms trembling as he rose, bearing his weight. Eyes large and alien behind thick glasses. His hawkish nose, hair combed back, always in a dress shirt, always in suit pants. Kathy unpredictable and sleepless, with her nervous hands and bulky body, talking in a neurotic stream. Raising her voice in euphoria or anger, or medicated into a lull. Kathy kept like a heart-shaped locket by a woman who had no heart, hung around her neck.

And Uncle Al, tall and lanky with a gait that swooped out on itself so that he always looked like he was moving to music. Glasses smeared and black greasy hair and eyes that didn't see. Ragged jeans and ragged sneakers and old T-shirts he'd had for years. He owned two electric guitars he didn't know how to play. He was always waving a cigarette, taking long needful drags or flicking the ash into the sink, his fingers moving emptily once stubbing one out until another was lit.

Al went away to college for a year and when he came back, his mind wasn't right. My grandmother liked to say that college ruined him. The one time he brought home a girlfriend, she was grotesquely overweight and wore bright pink lipstick and had rotten teeth and long ungroomed hair and she laughed too loudly at things that weren't funny, and everyone was glad when she never came back.

I was afraid of their stories, because they were stories left untold. Of my Uncle Jimmy going after his wife with a kitchen knife, of Kathy trying to die by jumping in front of a train. Of Tommy coming like a savior to rescue her from this very house, only to do her further damage in the end.

On the wall, the framed photograph of Kathy in her wedding gown, the one where she is kneeling down, gazing at the bouquet of flowers. The edges of her face softened for effect. The picture had faded from exposure to sun.

Down the hall, a master bedroom. In that bedroom, next to the large bed of my grandparents, a divider splitting off a separate space the exact width of a twin bed. Beside the bed, three shelves filled with stuffed animals. My aunt's room from when she was a girl. The sheets and bedclothes were plain. There was no window. There was a single crucifix on the wall. There was a curtain hanging open along the bottom of the bed that could be pulled along the rail, for privacy, as there was no door.

FLOWER GIRL

I held a basket lined with linen, gripped in one cotton glove with a mother-of-pearl snap at the wrist. I remember the potent scent; holding it was like pouring vanilla's inky extract into an otherwise odorless ingredient mix, or being the first out in the rain as each drop broke open to free its molecule of dust. The petals I let go seemed to molt powder like the bodies of moths. They lingered at my fingertips like lipstick marks, or beaded necklaces at a swan's throat, and drifted to the aisle's runner like a fairy tale's needle-pricked drops of blood on the snow. They feathered together to sweep before the edges of gowns; they were fleeting like breezes and whispered to the ground; they were wave froth the winds scattered; they were mouth-shaped stains scarlet to their cores.

I let petals drop before the hems of dresses, before the delicate arches of stocking-lined shoes, I threaded the sift and trickle of petals down before the feet of the bridesmaids and the father of the bride. Rose petals like breath proliferated out from my hand. Pink and red and white like the arteries of lovers. Their lacings like a scratch at the neck.

They were letters filled with secrets, confetti thrown to celebrate a year gone—they had the voicelessness of petticoats and of women holding their breath in church. They fell like autumn leaves, willowing like tongues along the starch and sheen of a slow march playing, like tendrils set in place with baby's breath, suggesting the false recital in a goodbye summer kiss.

In ancient Rome, I would have been carrying herbs and sheaths of wheat; in Elizabethan times, a ribboned bride's cup of silver and a gilded rosemary branch.

I imagined the petals could overrun the church, flow into the streets, snake into the gutters and brim the vestibules of buildings and the gaps in chandeliers with their gorgeous bleed, a river in Egypt, a pelt of small sighings and flitters like an insect's wing. I thought that crows could gather to snatch up their glitter. I thought they might be carried out to sea, to sing there like storm runoff in a gutter drain, or school like licks of flame. I wondered whether they would go brown as cut fruit marked with blight, whether they would spiral down like snow with its doll-skin porcelain or twine like ivies at our feet.

Kathy as a bride was a mirage I could hardly believe in: wrists like the rims of china teacups, skin like a bone-dust vase, eyes desolate as amber, a structure to her face like the carved museum torso of an ancient god. Her hair fell down her back with the sheen of a fine mink stole, and a smile harnessed the wattage coming off her chaste-white teeth.

I knew nothing about love. I was five years old. I remember Uncle Tommy's blue eyes and slight grin, his high Arabic cheekbones and lean toward one hip. My mother had said he was older and had fought in Vietnam. She said he had sent bouquets of flowers until they filled my grandmother's house, lilies and daisies and orchids and roses. He would take me around the block on the back of his motorcycle while my mother frowned and crossed her arms from the sidewalk, and for rides in a golden car we called a rocket ship. But I could not know what would come.

Once, girls had carried flowers before a coffin as well as before a bride.

I remember moving past those tightly sardined in the pews. Unfamiliar women who would later make a fuss over me and leave lipstick marks on my cheeks, women who were now leaning forward at the waist, smelling strongly of perfume, sweating slightly, bending in to snap my picture while smiling false smiles. Great-aunts with thick glasses and beauty parlor hair, half cousins with stylishly cut black leather jackets and pomaded curls, family friends with trim figures and flower print wrap-around dresses and tightly knotted belts. Everyone laughed and wore dark shades of eye shadow and smoothly shaven faces. The women's purses were sewn with sequins and taffeta and the pews had the deep shine of wood that has been recently buffed.

I remember dancing with my cousins. I remember Kathy posing for pictures under the dim light of the living room lamp, and her wedding dress left in an empty room, hanging from the top of a half-open door.

The dress resembled one of those Easter eggs with scenes inside. Delicate, intricate, the hardened icing swirled into lines and flourishes and frills, garish on the outer surface, with a peephole exposing a whole other world. Ducks suspended in ponds, rabbits nibbling grass, all backlit by the egg's translucence, its magnificent, churchlike glow.

I think now the scene inside must have been a kitchen. At the miniature table, a miniature woman sat with her hands on the table before her. Across from her, a miniature man. They were sharing a meal. The woman wore the small square cloth of an apron. Both were smiling. And while the egg itself was temporary, much like this dress meant to be worn for a single day, the scene inside was timeless. The figures were glued in place and would not change. You could look in on them and everything would remain the same.

Or maybe there was another scene, a different scene, not at all like the other. In it, a girl sat in her bedroom, if it could be called a bedroom. Not even a room really, just a wall divider splitting off a space the exact width of a twin-sized bed. Barely large enough to fit the girl inside. So tiny it was hardly real.

THE REPAIRS

I'd thought it was a good idea to buy a house, but a house is always a thing in need of repairs.

The pump on the well burned out. The element on the hot water heater went. The motor to the dryer snapped a belt. There was a scrape on the finish of the kitchen floor where someone dragged a table from one room to the next.

The thermostat misjudged the temperature of the room. The shrubbery needed to be pruned. The gutters filled with fallen leaves. The concrete crumbled from the steps of the stoop.

I remembered that when my grandparents died, mere months passed before their rent-controlled apartment had been split into two apartments. The cut-glass doorknobs were gone. The small strung bouzouki propped in the breakfront was gone. The heart-shaped jewelry my grandfather had made from the debris of a kamikaze plane was gone. The plastic on the couch was off. The same cracks in the back room ceiling. The same cars traveling the streets. The same plant tended by strangers could be seen from the kitchen window. Across the courtyard walled in by brick, where the lit angles slanted and the corners were always murky and dim and the television antenna cast a shadow like a crucifix, like the mast on a sinking ship.

Still, the history of an old house comes back.

When I didn't want to get out of bed, my mother would pull me up and push me into the bathroom and hold the door shut.

When I could not walk to the bathroom because of appendicitis, my mother dragged me out of bed by one arm, saying, *Of course you can walk!* So I kept the secret of my illness all night, piling the soiled sheets in the corner, lying on the bare mattress. My mother came in the morning and drew in her breath and we finally drove to the hospital just in time because I would have died if another hour had gone by and I had not been seen.

I split my head open on the coffee table and was driven to the hospital in the front seat. I remember there was blood on my panda bear; I remember being close to the windshield. I remember trying to touch a butterfly's wing. I remember a dream of a red mitten resting in the snow.

I thought mourning doves were owls for the longest time. They were hidden in the branches of the thick firs by the edge of the stream, and they would fly down individually and lift up in pairs. The whistling of their wings. When I found out my childhood house would be sold, I took pictures of the stream, but could never capture the ripples of the ducks in the light of it at dawn, or the way the leaves all fell or the way the snow draped over it or the way we had buried my parakeet under the crabapple tree that the new owners would someday cut down. As she dug a hole, my mother's gray high heels in the rain. The heels said, *I have to go to work. I do not want to bury your bird.* The heels down the hallway to my room said, *You do not have a fever, you are not really sick.*

The place where someone long ago spilled a gallon of paint on the indoor-outdoor rug in the sunroom, a white matted stain with a cut square of carpet covering it up.

We tried to have a garden once. Did we? No. We had lilacs and oaks. We had a hammock once between the two trees where I dreamed a child was buried. A child was buried there. Someone's stillborn. I only found out once we had moved.

Meanwhile, air knocked in the heating pipes. The water main broke.

The hole in the roof. The leak from the ice dam. The water running from the ceiling down onto the floor. The shower curtain taped to the window to direct it into the sink.

My mother's husband reads the newspaper in an old chair by the fire, at the dinner table, standing in the kitchen, sitting down to lunch. When he skis, he calculates in his head as he rides the lift how much each run will cost. He owns an old Mercedes that he bought from a dead man's girlfriend. He went to the house and wrote a check and took the keys and drove it out of the garage. He had a moustache for forty years after his father died. He had a swimming pool with his second wife.

The water damage. Mildew damage. Mice chewing the wires, chewing the wood. Ant infestation. Failure of a pilot light in the furnace to ignite.

My mother said, *Screw you, you bitch* and drove to a vacation on Cape Cod without me after ordering me to take my packed bags out of the trunk. After taking out the bags herself and leaving them there on the lawn.

My father threw out a gallon of wine that week while I was staying at his apartment, sleeping on the foldout bed in the living room. Watching the small TV on a wheeled cart all day while he was at work. I took the wine from the dumpster and drank it until it made me sick.

The septic system overflowed so that when the toilet flushed the sewage came up through the shower drain.

When I gave birth, I remember screaming and wondering what I heard, whose untethered voice.

Gaps at the windows. Knicks in the floor. Split wood weakening the silverware drawer. Formica marred by knives missing the cutting board.

I would watch the zebras at the zoo swatting their tails and stitching their skin a bit at the shoulder to ward off flies. Clustering in the shade. Gulping steep drinks from the trough. Nibbling in a non-committal way at the grass. Skin crosshatched by the chainlink fence and the shadowed afternoon. Their manes sparse. Their eyes like stagnant water at the head of a stream. That, and the long days all the same stretching before them. Driving them insane.

The sinkhole the septic system makes in the yard and what it will cost to repair. The radon filter and the plasma TV, and the coffee table with the watermark from the glass filled with beer when I forgot how much the condensation would bleed.

THE ACCIDENTS

O ne summer night before I left for college, we drove to the fairgrounds and parked. As we pulled in, the concrete wall's familiar graffiti rose up in the headlights of my father's car. We parked
alongside the wall and Harry lifted me and carried me like a bride toward the threshold of the tall chain-link fence, and, after climbing it
and jumping to the far side, we lay in the darkness together beneath
the stars, taking in breath and letting out breath. The grass with its
little spears made me aware of my body, the cool sparse stalks, the
almost-chill of the end-of-summer air. Then he was above me, kissing me, whispering, *This is the moment.* Telling me he loved me. But I
knew deep inside myself that there was something different waiting,
turning me into someone else.

I felt the night inside me like knives, like gears, playing like a
radio song where parents vanish and vehicles leave their tracks and
illegal substances are taken and tobacco smoke is inhaled, where
cheap beers are sipped from silver cans and pool balls bump against
rubber and plush. I breathed out into the night, into a sky that
couldn't know I was there, about to leave for a life that could hardly
be imagined now that the life I had thought was mine had melted
away like a snowcap and not like a candle, with no purpose or light
or warmth. No wick, just a slow evaporation I hadn't seen until

the day it was over, gone, and the brown peak of some summit was exposed.

A year before, I had followed Harry to another girl's house to prove to myself he was cheating and broken up with him on the lawn.

Months from now, I would be arrested for a felony I hadn't known I had committed, and would only avoid jail time because my father pushed his way through the four policemen working to restrain him and shouted through their chokehold *Don't sign anything!* as my pen was poised over the signature line.

Harry was also a young man addicted to what he had become. He loved to drop acid at the pool hall. He loved to drive his trucks into trees. He loved to walk away with others' things. He loved to drink in the fields of the fairgrounds and have sex with girls in the backs of their cars, driving drunk or under the influence of pot or some other drug; he loved it all, it fed some flame in him and kept him warm. He was invincible. He loved the slow suicide of it, because he continued to beat the odds.

I was always battling time, looking for the weakness in it, trying to find or make rips or holes that I could slip through for an extra hour when my mother wasn't questioning where I was. I would sneak out of my high school internship, lie and say I was going to the movies. I would move along its seams seeking a gap I could slip through and disappear. I would rush down that same road by the old mill to his house and he would be there working on his old Monte Carlo that didn't run or he would come out to meet me as I pulled up.

Hey, Skid.

I would move over, he would slip into the driver's seat and take the car off the road into the muddy woods and spin the tires and aim its great yellow bulk through the bare-throated trees. He would drive the car beyond what it could do and I would smell rubber and cringe in the passenger seat and ask him to slow down in a voice that sounded afraid and weak. Once he drove so recklessly he tore a hole in the muffler so that the car revved loudly and stalled out each time I drove and I had to replace the exhaust system. Once in the city, he realized he was driving the wrong way down a one-way street and so slung his arm across the long vinyl back of the seat and turned around to see while he reversed, but went so fast that he smashed the headlights on one car and scratched another down the side and then turned down another street and promptly drove off. The whole way home I looked at the stump where my side view mirror had been.

When my mother saw my missing mirror, I told her I had been the one driving during the accident, and she took me to the police station in Providence to report it. We sat for an hour parked in a meter spot until I won the battle by refusing to get out.

It went on until the day Harry and I were headed someplace and the engine started to smoke, white vapor pouring out of the rear exhaust, and he kept driving though I said we should stop, the car was overheating, the car was overheating. He kept on until the car couldn't go anymore and the head was cracked from the heat and then I had no car.

I was no stranger to accidents. The first day I got my driver's license, I drove my father's car to the shopping plaza I had always walked to, just because I could. I wanted to drive to McDonald's for lunch, though the McDonald's was only three doors down. As I pulled out, leaning back over the seat to see behind me, I heard a sound like the crumpling of an empty beer can. I had hit the car parked beside me. Mr. Albro, my driving teacher, had taught me much, but he had not taught me that I had to watch the front end of my car while backing out of a spot. My father's car ended up wedged in the crease I'd made in the other car's passenger door and I could not get it free no matter how I maneuvered. I called my parents. The police came. The car ended up belonging to Dawn McAlister's mother. I went to school with Dawn, and my parents paid her parents $350 in cash, the cost of repairs, to keep the insurance companies out of it. I saw the family drive by in the car years later and the dent still hadn't been repaired.

I hit cars. I hit trucks. I once totaled a car a week after I'd bought it. I drove my father's car over concrete blocks that had fallen into the road and flattened three of the tires, then drove on the rims until they were bent beyond repair. I hit a parked truck when I turned to wave at Harry's best friend as he walked along the sidewalk one afternoon, and then I drove to Harry's house where he tried to bang out the dent. My first car had streaks of paint to prove what I'd done. Blue paint. Grey paint. White from where I'd scraped against the concrete pillar at the gas station.

Once, after a party in the woods, I drove through a red light. It was at a major intersection, and the car that hit me was moving fast enough to take my front bumper entirely off. Someone who was sitting in the back-seat, a friend of a friend, said I should just leave. My friend pointed out that my front license plate was now lying in the road. When the police came, they realized that two of the people in my car were runaways, and one was wanted on a warrant for his arrest. I put the bumper in my trunk and carried it into my father's living room when I got to his apartment that night.

There were also accidents that should have happened, but didn't. The time Jimmy Cole drove drunk in his pickup over the rough hills under the powerlines with me in the passenger seat. The ride I took in the car of a boy I didn't know while he drove drunk down pitch-black back-woods roads at eighty miles per hour with the headlights off, to prove how well he knew the twists and turns. The time Harry passed another car on the too-narrow and too-steep lanes of the old Jamestown Bridge. He leaned over to kiss me while we were in the lane for oncoming cars. I leaned away and told him we would die. A few years later they built a new bridge right beside the old one, and I remembered seeing the dark water beneath the open gaps between slabs of road.

Greg Getchell would die in a motorcycle accident. Buddha Jackson would die from cirrhosis of the liver. Eddie Corbett would die in the nightclub fire. No one could have told me that then.

Harry's younger brother would die. His older stepbrother would die as well.

Harry himself would be dead.

Everything would go as Harry was going now. Without there being any way of knowing or saying or putting one's thumb right on the place and feeling the going together so that it didn't or wouldn't hurt. Slowly, the shared hours of my life would vanish away, fade because I could not hold onto the others who made those experiences complete. The Egyptian mummy made from papier-mâché in the fourth grade. How Mr. McCollough had defended me missing class to play the violin in fifth. Conversations on rooftops and bowling alley crushes and long talks over old books and cheap wine, all gone, gone, gone.

But how was I to know. Here. Now. Seventeen years old in a field just off a main road with a boy a year younger than me. Both feeling grown, like life had come, not knowing we were not even solid shapes, that we would change and become whatever the world wanted from us. That in the coming years we would not understand how it had come to this, whatever little groove we had worn ourselves into, and we would think back on this night when the air was cold and the stars were high and the thin cirrus clouds scuttered their barely-there rudderless boats: we would know this too late. I would get back into my father's car with its cracked dashboard and stuffing coming out of the seats, the very metaphor for my father's life, and Harry would walk back into the empty kitchen of a house where half of love was half neglect, the dingy, smoke-filled living rooms with a stepfather you didn't want to disturb passed out on the couch, the bedroom with a bare mattress and flimsy presswood door, the kind men could put a fist through and would. He might shut the kitchen cabinet a bit too abruptly as a way of saying goodbye to a girl he would hardly remember through the haze of later years. Maybe Harry had loved me for a brief time in the way he did, but what was there to do but walk away. He would not be hurt. He would kiss me again in the grass years later, but we couldn't know that now. It was his job to walk out of my life as I moved on to a future without him.

Conspiracy to
Commit Larceny

"Sign the paper and I can tell you what's going on."

I looked at the form on the table before me, skimmed its contents briefly, and signed.

"So you know why you're here?" He leaned back in his chair now and rested his hands behind his head.

I nodded.

"We know about what happened. We've talked to both Harry and Joe. They gave us your name."

I shifted forward in the hard chair.

"Do you have anything you want to tell us?"

I'd done nothing wrong, so the story was easy to tell. How we'd driven to the neighborhood, how the two of them had disappeared into the dark outside the car, how they had returned with a cell phone and a radar detector, how I'd dropped them off at someone's house.

"Did you know the items were stolen?"

I paused.

"I had an idea, I guess, from the way they talked."

The officer rolled his chair back then and started to type. "I just want to get this all down," he said.

I was happy to help. They were the police, after all. Long en-trenched lessons of elementary school and after-school programs had taught me: these officers were my friends.

When he was done typing, he placed the sheet of paper on the table before me and asked me to read it over to be sure it was right.

"Then you can sign at the bottom."

I read the statement carefully and picked up the pen.

Then I heard a commotion out in the hall. Someone was shout-ing, and trying to get down the corridor. I thought I recognized my father's voice. Then his head appeared, straining to see over the arms of four police officers holding him back.

"Has she been arrested?" It was almost a growl and almost a sob.

I heard one of the men in the hall say yes.

Afterward, I would be led out. I would protest that I hadn't been read my rights. I would be fingerprinted by a different officer. I would feel the urge to smile when the mug shot was taken.

I would be taken to a room with a two-way mirror and a marred wooden bench. My belt and shoes would be taken from me. I would wonder who was watching me from behind the hollow glass.

As I sat, I would look at the marks on the bench. Into the surface of the wood, endless names had been carved. *Someone isn't doing a very good job at confiscating sharp objects*, was my first thought. Then I ran my fingers over the names. The wood rough, the ink fading in some places, and in others, dark and clear. It occurred to me that attached to every name here was a person who had committed a crime. What had happened to these peo-ple? Were they lifelong criminals? Were they in prison now? Were some of them dead?

I would find out in the weeks to come that I was the only one of the three of us involved that night who was eighteen, old enough to be jailed. That the police wanted an arrest for this and that they wanted it to be me. I couldn't know that it was a crime to drive the car and know a crime had happened and not report it.

I would find out that Harry and Joe hadn't actually given the police my name, and had said I knew nothing about what happened. That the police had lied.

And I would find out that signing the statement I'd given to the police would have been the one thing that could send me to jail.

I was under arrest, literally under. Like being under a spell, or under a heavy object weighted down. I was stopped. I was halted. I was kept from. I could not walk out if I wanted to.

I should have explained to the cops that they'd made a mistake. That I was not one of *them*. Except, I now realized, all that made them *them* was their actions.

I was confused, and on the verge of tears. They were the law. They were the good guys. They were the ones with the shiny stars and high leather boots and kind faces. But I knew better now. They had fooled me because they wanted to arrest me. I was the criminal to them.

I saw what was behind the officer's eyes now. I saw all the official distance that I had not seen before. His shorn hair. His strict jaw. I saw his eyes, eyes that let nothing in. Eyes that would deceive a child to be able to prosecute a case. Except that I was technically now an adult in the eyes of the law.

"Sir, if you don't back off and leave peacefully right now, you'll be arrested as well."

As my father's face disappeared, as they managed to get some leverage and pull him out, he pushed back with a last burst of will and yelled to me.

"Jen! Don't sign anything!"

And with that he was gone.

THE DEATHS

"You can't lose your glasses, Lou. You must not lose them. Here, give them to me."

These were the words my grandmother had for my grandfather as he lay on his deathbed.

"You can't leave tissues all over the bed, Lou. We're not at home. You can't pull all the tissues out of the box."

He spent his final hours blind, without anything to catch the phlegm he couldn't quite cough up.

He also asked about the ice.

When I had first filled the Styrofoam cup with ice chips from the machine down the hall and shimmied them into his mouth, he looked at me through murky eyes and a kind of wonder crossed his face. He had whispered something, a mere rasp at the back of his throat.

"What?" I leaned in closer.

With my ear to his mouth, I could just make out his words: "How much does the ice cost?"

Now he lay there, a constant relentless gargle in his throat. His hair was thick and white and combed back from his face. His fingers trembled. I didn't touch his hand. Then I did. I sat quietly. I strained not to talk.

Parkinson's had been erasing him for years. I realized that when I remembered him, I would remember him as a ghost in the living room, in the corner recliner asleep. He did not forget our names because he never spoke our names. He didn't talk about the past because he didn't talk about the present. He was simply a hollow vessel waiting.

My father sat awkwardly on the other side of the room. What was there to do? We would sit for hours and then go home. We would say little. My grandmother would find ways to scold my grandfather for dying in such an inconvenient way. She stood at the foot of the bed without touching him, her arms folded across her chest, a gesture that cut her off, like a road bulldozed or a drawbridge raised.

"So how are things?" my father would finally ask.

I would glance over to read the look on his face.

"Fine," I answered, unwilling to make small talk over my grandfather as though he weren't there, wasting away beneath the sheets. My father seemed careless, but maybe he cared. Maybe he cared too much. Maybe he needed to fill the room with sound, with his meaningless words; maybe he was working like a bird with marbles or stones to slowly get the water level to rise. Word by word, he was filling the empty jar of the room. He was doing it to keep himself afloat.

I looked at my grandfather again. What did he think there? Did he remember? No, he could not remember. Did he dream? No, he could not dream. His trembling hands led him to the bottoms of his brain where the limbo lay. There was no good. There was no bad. There was just the mild white landscape and the faceless nurses with their sharp or tender voices. There was just the medication and the check of the vitals. There was the catheter bag filling. What can be as empty as waiting for death?

"No," he said, without knowing he had said anything. His lips went slack. He drew in air. The room had no warmth. It had no clock. He had no time. He could hear footsteps in the hall. He could feel his catheter empty. He could feel his bladder drain. He did not know what it meant.

I remember him cranking the awning above the patio closed so it would not be caught in the wind. I remember him driving to the bakery in their broad old car with the broken grate at the front and the one small dent in the fender. I remember him pulling up to the garage door and backing the car out slowly. He would bring home rolls in a roped white box with the bakery string that outdid the strength of his hands. He would edge up the avenue and wait long for the light and turn down under the el and park after four attempts to back into a space. He would park too close to the hydrant and take his chances and then shuffle down the block. He would watch the tissue wrap the baked goods. He would look at his watch.

Once home, he would sink into the corner recliner, as though the chair were a coat rack where he could hang up his body like a trenchcoat or a hat. He would sit and drift off. He would sleep on and off and let the day go. There was nothing to do but nod off until dinner, there was nothing to do but doze and let the mouth fall open and let the head nod forward and let the hands grip the armrests lightly until dinner came, and the day was over and the hours could pass in sleep.

At the funeral, there was no burial. I remember standing in the early spring air as geese fed in the fields around the graves. The stone was there with his name on it, but the ground needed to thaw.

At the service, lines of somber, suited men bowed their heads, making the sign of the cross. My grandfather's mouth was sewn shut.

When a baby started to cry behind me, I imagined my grandfather as a baby. I wondered whether there was anyone in the room who could remember the moment he was born.

My father told me he had gone to see Kathy just before, to give her the news. She would have sat, awkwardly overweight, with patches of dark facial hair and a sheen of perspiration at her brow. An oversized purse looped over her shoulder as she clutched its shapeless bulk to her chest. She would have thrown up her hands when she saw my father, and smiled widely, so that he could see a gap where she'd lost another tooth.

"Joey, I'm so glad you're here! I'm *so* happy!" Her tone out of whack. Lilting, rising, the strange over-the-top way she had when she was up.

He would have said, "We need to talk."

She would have sat with difficulty on the edge of the cot. She would have breathed heavily through her mouth. He wouldn't have known how to tell her. He wouldn't have known how she'd react. And then: "Dad's dead."

Her face must have changed, aged, and she would have reached into her bag and started rummaging through it. Various items withdrawn and placed on the bed before her. A nubby hairbrush. Elastics. Band-Aids. A shabby wallet with a broken clasp. Finally, a crushed pack of cigarettes with a lighter tucked in at the top.

She would have tapped out a cigarette and said she wasn't going to the funeral. She would have gone outside to smoke.

Among other residents milling about on the front walkway, mumbling, smoking, staring blankly into space, she would have held her cigarette to the lighter and taken a long drag. Exhaled the smoke and dropped her hand to her side.

"Now it's just mom, isn't it? And us." She would have grabbed his arm and pulled him close.

"Maybe when mom goes," she may have whispered, "don't come and tell me." Grinned a bit until he could smell the smoke on her breath. "Maybe I just don't want to know."

My grandfather's brother sat at the front of the room during the funeral, perhaps remembering himself and his brother as boys, their skinny arms and dirty white shirts and the laundry hung on the line. The way Lou was the quiet one, the sad one, but the one who dressed the best. Maybe he remembered my grandfather's wedding to my grandmother and her laughing like glass and the magnificent gown and his brother's skinny long nose and cowlick hair and cocked hat. How they danced and drank. Maybe he remembered the olive trees in the yard and their thick mother with her long hair pinned up and the severe dinners with the broken bread and the old heavy plates and the firm mouth of his mother and the shined shoes of his father. Maybe he remembered chasing the pigeons on the boardwalk at Coney Island. Watching his brother run before him. The sound of his shoes still there in his mind. Each falling, a cold rhythm. Like the ticking of a clock.

My grandmother sat beside him, facing forward. She had the expression of someone watching the inevitable destruction of men. Her profile was the profile of a god.

The last time I saw my grandmother, her hair had gone white, and she cried as our visit ended. I noticed her shoulders shaking before I heard the faint sobs.

"I hate goodbyes. I hate them. They are too sad, too sad."

The crying gained momentum. My father froze. His mother was the kind of woman who was always in control. He had never seen her cry. He patted her lightly on the back, the way people handle children when they don't like children.

"We'll be back, Mom. Don't worry. It's not goodbye, we'll be back soon."

And then we were out the door. I knew she was still sitting at the kitchen table, crying alone. I asked if we should stay. My father said, "We'll stay longer next time. She'll be fine."

The next time I saw her, she was lying in a coffin. Her hair was black again. She had stopped eating and starved herself to death.

"Let me get a picture of you two!" my father had said just an hour before we left.

My grandmother sighed and threw up her hands meekly, then returned them to their grip on the handles of her wheelchair. She reached out to arrange the already-squeezed lemon on the saucer before her, she fiddled with the edge of her folded napkin, she flipped at the tab on the tea bag, she gingerly sipped her tea. The clock ticked, a long shadow of individual audible knits in the longer stitches of minutes going by.

I posed beside my grandmother's chair and placed a hand on her shoulder. I could see her freckles and her graying but beautiful teeth.

"Smile!" my father said. We smiled. I could feel the thin cotton and jutting shoulder blades under my hand, could see the hollow between the bones of her wrist and the gnarl of the hands which were once delicate.

The camera clicked and clicked again.

Before starting up the car, my father pulled out his camera. It made a happy chirping noise when he turned it on. He had bought it recently and had been talking about how easy it was to take pictures. No fuss. Just press the button and a picture appeared in the screen. He flipped through the pictures he'd taken.

"These are great! They came out so good!" he exclaimed. He lifted the camera so I could get a glimpse. In one he took of me standing with his mother, she looked bright, happy, almost youthful, as if she was remembering something that had happened long ago and smiled for that moment instead of for this one.

As he passed through the photos, the camera beeped again and again, and he began deleting pictures that were blurry or dark. There was a button with a trash can symbol on it and he pressed it. The device beeped and he pressed the trash can again. The screen went black. He pressed the arrow that led to the next picture. Black. He pressed again. No image.

As he pressed the button again and again, and listened to the camera beep emptily, I heard him make a noise deep in his throat. He turned to me, distraught.

"I can't believe I did it. I didn't mean to. How did I do that?"

"What?" I asked.

"I erased them. I erased them all."

KNOCK WOOD

In the end, I recognized that the train approaching was not the one that had dropped me off. I recognized the train tracks for what they were. Paths to different horizons. Arteries to a heart. In the end, it was the pressurized chamber, the burden of too much.

Who can ever have it all? Who can ever have what they want?

I had to be a person in the world. I had to function and mother and pay bills and go to work. I had to do more than be a ghost of all my desires and a person who could blur the future and the past. In the end, I had to be a happening no crystal ball could predict. I had to let the seagulls loose. I had to let the smoke fly up.

I felt it ending before I felt it end. I felt the smooth darkness coming like a plague of locusts or a death. I felt the rivers turn to blood. I felt God getting revenge on me while no one had my back.

Finally, I ran out of time. The déjà vus disappeared. I stopped remembering what had yet to come. I knew it was time to undo this self. I knew it was time to leap from the bridge. I told Tim, but he couldn't understand. He didn't want me to go. His mother had gone. In her last years, she had forgotten his name. I remembered she had touched my hair, and only panicked when we talked of death. After she was dead, the stain from her blood was still on the carpet, from when she had fallen and hit her head against the headboard. After she died, Tim sold her apartment because he could not go back.

I told him my going would not be like this, that all time happened at once. That I had to stop living on luck. That I had to stop borrowing moments I couldn't control, like a horse. I told him if he ever missed me, he would just have to go back through the wormholes where we lived, to the moments. They were always there, discarded like newspapers in the park. Kept like the baby teeth of children in a box. Kept like mummies, carefully wrapped. He would always have me. Though *always* was a farce.

I wondered if he wanted to kill me and hide away my body at that moment, or clip off and keep a lock of my hair. I could understand this impulse, like the iridescent dragonfly wings I had found in the long grass in France and pressed into the pages of a book.

To begin the process of my death, I had to understand it was a form of escape. I had to relive the moments that had been gardened into rows. I had to pull them up by the roots.

I took off my ring of wood. I wondered where the tree had grown, how thick it had been, what insects had lived beneath its bark, what caterpillars had gnawed its leaves. I wondered what shade it had given and what seeds it had dropped. I wondered at the circles the branches would have made as they grew out. Knots tied and untied, knots like eyes with which to watch.

I took off my ring. Then I knocked. I knocked on metal, I knocked on glass. I knocked on the still surface of a mirror. I knocked on pavement. I knocked on my fingernails and the enamel of my teeth. I accumulated so much filth and trouble in the future and past. I felt the blanket of space-time that rested tranquil between the planets bunch. I felt my parallel selves in other universes stir and gape. I plainly felt myself go. I wouldn't be. I wouldn't know. All the time happening at once would cease and I would be erased. I gave in and I gave up. I couldn't be with Tim and I couldn't be without. I couldn't betray the people I loved. I couldn't betray myself. So I stepped to the edge and stepped off. Until I wasn't anymore.

Tim tried to stop me, but he could only watch. Maybe he remembered how he had found me on the train platform at 2 a.m., a vagabond, a drunk. Maybe he was remembering the first words he had said to me. Maybe he was remembering the future. I knew he would keep all the best me's intact. And for this reason I knew I had made the right choice. No me in the present moment could be as perfect as me in the past. I had to die like my uncle and like my aunt. We were all dead already. We were all just being born. Memory was the only ribbon sealing the package. It was time for the knot of mine to be pulled loose. And so I pulled.

In that moment, I saw his face, in all its grief. So many lines, it was a thread I could follow back to his door, or a map I could follow back to my own. Caverns with rivers. Galaxies with gaseous clouds. Cracks in the vase that has yet to crumble, but has already begun to leak. In his face was the death of Harry, the heroin in his vein. A crime to be committed. A rabbit pelt hung in the yard. In his face, Joe's black eye and broken teeth. Tim carried a sadness that was the revolving glass door to that first Manhattan hotel. A subway passing, the one that had murmured underground the day I found myself across from that same hotel, by chance. Subway going in the opposite direction from the way I walked. I could feel time stringing out in both directions before me. I had been holding onto my children that afternoon, one by each hand.

Then I was at the station. It was that first June day, the day of my arrival and our meeting years before. The train had returned and was waiting so that I could get on. The knuckle with which I knocked turned to dust. My mother's proteins unstitched. Those few strands I had been dissolved. My mother's mother became unborn. My father's father returned to a single cell. Spartans who were my ancestors rose from their graves. The universe glinted. I remembered. I forgot. I stepped from the platform. Then there were none.

Vow

When her daughter got married, Kathy showed up at the church. No one had expected it; no one even recognized her at first. Just as the couple turned back to the priest so he could pronounce them man and wife, I heard the heavy wooden doors to the street creak open. A square of light stretched down the aisle. A woman was shuffling in, wearing a worn coat and oversized clothes and thick shoes. She looked like a homeless person taking refuge from the cold.

She lumbered around the back of the rows and lowered herself into the final seat of the final pew. She made the sign of the cross and maneuvered herself to her knees and rested her hands on the seat back before her. Her eyes were shining as though she had seen God.

She would have been seeing her daughter as she was seventeen years before, riding the carousel at Nellie Bly, laughing, hair pinned back from her face with ribbon barrettes. Chocolate ice cream at the corners of her mouth and drying down the front of her shirt. Walking back to the car once the ride was over, Kathy would have registered the stares of strangers passing. She imagined how the two of them must look through the eyes of others: Kathy imagined how she appeared, her feet crammed into black flats, her forehead clammy with sweat, tendrils of hair sticking to the sides of her face, a cigarette burning in her hand with its long curl of ash, lumbering beside the delicate, blue-eyed wisp of a girl. She could hardly walk. Her breath wheezed and creaked. What would her daughter do without her around if anything ever happened?

Then she had begun to see—almost against her will—a different possibility take shape. Even now, as her daughter was looking up at her happily, worshipfully. And it struck her: in her absence, her daughter, the one person she loved without question or reserve, would have a better chance at a normal life. At that moment, she had perhaps decided. She would have herself committed.

She would go to the asylum for good, and her parents would care for her daughter better than she could.

And now here was that daughter, walking down the aisle, a married woman, a wife, moving to the door. As soon as the two emerged, guests would throw birdseed and the bride would duck her head. Her bouquet would lift. Her veil would stream behind her as she ran down the stairs, her hand in her new husband's hand. The lace of the veil would fill with wind, would shimmer out and expand like water; it would lift, it was so light. The bride's smile would reflect in the car's waxed surface as they approached, as they stooped down into the black antique with its hood like the prow of a boat, with the white shoe polish that spelled *Just Married* sprawled across the rear windshield and tin cans tied off the back.

Kathy remembered her wedding to Tommy, how he stood at the end of the aisle in his platform shoes and the white suit with the ruffled tuxedo shirt, with his decisive Arabic nose and slanting, mysterious smile and lovely skin, not suntanned, but allowing her to imagine him in the sun. How he used to come on his motorcycle with flowers in his hand, lilies or orchids or roses or daisies, how he would slide her onto the bike behind him, put her arms around his waist, and ride her off, her black hair spitting sharply into her face, his own hair flying in a wild tangle of speed. They would ride under the el and along the parkway. They would drive to Coney Island and order hot dogs. They boarded the ferris wheel and let it lift them until she could see, far below, the sand meet the ocean, the ocean meet the sky. How he had gotten down on one knee before her when he proposed, asking, "Will you marry me?" an air of sadness about him even then, and she felt the whole world holding its breath before she said, "Tommy. Yes! Of course."

Now the car holding her daughter would pull out from the curb, this automobile with an engine like a horse, and all the newlyweds' hope alive in it as they moved away from the crowd, waving and waving from this sturdy ship, this old car that would carry them, carry them forth.

ACKNOWLEDGMENTS

Grateful acknowledgment is made to the editors of the following journals, in which these essays first appeared:

The Collagist: "The Repairs"
Mid-American Review: "Invasive Species," "The Problems of the
    Mothers," "Dear Your Honor:"
Tupelo Quarterly: "On Time"
Verse: "The Mechanics"

The essay "A Beautiful Housing of Epidemics," which included the essays "The Witnesses," "Duplex," and "Vow," was named a finalist for the 2017 *New Letters* Prize for Nonfiction.

For friendship, influence, and advice, thank you to Andre Dubus III, Julianna Baggott, Jeff Friedman, Lily Hoang, Tim Liardet, Maura MacNeil, Andrew Morgan, David Ryan, and Allison Titus. Thank you as well to everyone at Dzanc Books, especially to Michelle Dotter, who has had a tremendous hand in making this book what it is.